Tricia Goyer has walked the ___
and is full of hope, con___
only will help teen m___
grandparents, friends, ___
ten with compassion, ___
ing, and encouraging. ___
young moms and give ___

—Courtney Jo___
WomenLivingWell.org and GoodMorningGirls.org

Tricia Goyer has done it again! Teen Mom not only takes us on a rollercoaster ride of teen moms' experiences, but she makes one point crystal clear: that the way you start has nothing to do with the way you end. This book encourages women of all ages, letting them know that it's never too late to have a bright future.

—Angelia White, CEO and founder, *Hope for Women* magazine

Teen Mom, your life is moving in a new direction now, a direction full of potential and purpose. Tricia Goyer has given you a beautiful gift between the covers of this book. I encourage you to unwrap it. All the inspiration and information you need is within these pages.

—Tracy Steel, speaker and author of *Images of His Beauty*, www.onedegreeministries.com

What I love most about *Teen Mom* is it's filled with wisdom and solid encouragement. I wish I'd had this book when I was twenty-one, pregnant, unmarried, and scared to death. Tricia's words are like a balm of reassurance for the young woman who can't see past the two lines on her pregnancy test.

—Erin Bishop, founder and president of the Whatever Girls

Those who work with teen moms know how difficult it is to find good resources, so it's great news to have this engaging, encouraging, challenging, and truthful book written about the issues that matter to young mothers. Finally, something just for them!

—Crystal Kirgiss, teacher, speaker, writer, and author of many books, including *More Than Skin Deep: A Guide to Self and Soul*

Love this book. Inspiring, poignant, sympathetic, and challenging. Tricia understands all the issues teen moms face, and she empowers them to own their role as mothers with faith, hope, and courage. All teen moms and mothers of these teens need this book. Highly recommended.

—Sally Clarkson, speaker, ministry leader, and author of numerous books, including *Desperate: Hope for the Mom Who Needs to Breathe*

Teen Mom

You're Stronger than You Think

TRICIA GOYER

Previously titled *Life Interrupted*

 ZONDERVAN®

ZONDERVAN

Teen Mom
Copyright © 2015 by Tricia Goyer

Previously titled *Life Interrupted*

This title is also available as a Zondervan ebook. Visit www.zondervan.com/ebooks.

Requests for information should be addressed to:
Zondervan, 3900 *Sparks Dr. SE, Grand Rapids, Michigan 49546*

This edition: 978-0-310-33887-1

Library of Congress Cataloging-in-Publication Data

Goyer, Tricia.
    Life interrupted : the scoop on being a young mom / Tricia Goyer.
      p. cm.
    Includes bibliographical references.
    ISBN-10: 0-310-25316-0
    ISBN-13: 978-0-310-25316-7
    1. Teenage mothers — Religious life. 2. Unmarried mothers — Religious life.
  I. Title.
    BV4529.18.G69 2004
    248.8'33 — dc22   2004004686

Published in association with Janet Kobobel Grant, Books & Such, 4788 Carissa Ave., Santa Rosa, CA 95405

Cover design and illustration: Connie Gabbert
Cover photography: ©vovan / Shutterstock®
Interior design and composition: Greg Johnson/Textbook Perfect

First printing January 2015 / Printed in the United States of America

To every young mom
who hopes for a good future.
You can do it. You matter!

What's Inside

Before I Was a Mom

Before I was a mom,
I spent every night with friends.
I texted for hours on the phone.
And I watched every decent Redbox movie.

Before I was a mom,
I stayed up all night.
Slept 'til noon on weekends.
Had my nails done.

Before I was a mom,
I did my homework … most of the time.
Knew all the Lady Gaga lyrics.
Watched TV that doesn't include puppets.

Before I was a mom,
I didn't realize the importance of nap time.
Didn't consider the danger of electrical outlets.
Spoke in complete sentences.

Before I was a mom,
I didn't wear spit-up on my shoulder.
Thought poop was disgusting.
Gagged at drool.
Never imagined sniffing a diaper.

Before I was a mom,
I had big plans for my future.
Looked into college.
Never considered the cost of day care.
Had no idea what *effaced* or *epidural* mean.

Before I was a mom,
I thought all babies look alike.
Didn't realize how exciting crawling can be.
Never thought to record someone walking.
Didn't know how beautiful *mama* sounds.

Before I was a mom,
I never watched a baby sleep.
Never appreciated a baby's soft giggle.
Never knew how much love I have inside.
Never thought one small being could change me so completely.

Before I was a mom,
I never realized a feeling so great,
So wonderful,
So intimate,

As loving my own child.

— Tricia Goyer

Me ... A Mom?

Growing up, did you imagine yourself as a mom? Did you plan for it, dream about it? Did you like the idea of having kids? I did. I loved kids, and I always thought I'd be a great mom, so why did I panic when I discovered my dream was coming true? Mostly because it was too soon. Way too soon. As a high schooler, I knew my life was about to change forever. And it did.

My Story

Each and every teen mom has her own story. Each and every teen mom has her own journey. My first child is twenty-five years old now, and I have a great, amazing life. But no matter what success I achieve, I'll never forget the moment that I found out I was going to have a baby.

Me? A mom? I'd always wanted a baby but never imagined it would happen at age seventeen.

Like most little girls, I imagined marrying an amazing guy and becoming a mom. In bed at night, I'd let my mind wander. I pictured my future family. I wanted lots of kids, and I thought I'd be a good mom. Since I didn't know my biological dad growing up—and my stepdad was distant and unconcerned about me—I wanted a husband who really cared about me and my kids.

I wanted to be a teacher, but I don't remember anyone talking to me about college. I got good grades, but there was so much happening in everyday life that I didn't really look ahead.

From a young age, I was obsessed with boys. I remember having crushes beginning in the fourth grade. I wasn't pretty, and I was awkward. When I was younger, I was a chubby kid with buckteeth. I envied my friends with their thin frames and nice clothes. I wanted boys to like me the way I liked them.

Then in seventh grade something happened. I started walking to and from school and playing basketball and volleyball. I lost weight. The summer before eighth grade, I liked a guy I'd met at the lake. He was in town for the summer, and he was my first kiss. He was sixteen, rich, drove his dad's speedboat, and had a motorcycle. It was like something from a movie. But then he left after the summer.

At the end of eighth grade, there was a new girl in school whose brother was tall and handsome. My friend told me he liked me, and I didn't believe it until I was staying over at her house and he kissed me. We started dating and things got physical. I was almost fourteen and didn't think much about getting pregnant. Thankfully, I didn't.

He moved away too, and I had other boyfriends. More than anything, I wanted to be loved, and in my searching, I found myself pregnant. I was in shock. I was only fifteen. I was afraid of anyone finding out, and I didn't want to go to school pregnant. My mom took me to a Planned Parenthood Clinic, and they told me that an abortion was the right choice. I agreed, mistakenly thinking it was the easy way out.

I dealt with the pain and heartache of my choice but soon became pregnant again. Same boyfriend, same concerns, but this time I knew I wanted to have my baby. I was seventeen.

I remember riding home from the doctor's office with my mom when I saw a familiar car heading the other direction. "There he is," I blurted. My boyfriend had another girl in his car. For the last four or five months, he'd been going between her and me. She was with him now, but I was going to have his baby.

My mom flipped a U-turn. We followed the dented Nova into the McDonald's parking lot.

I jumped out and marched to his car. "We need to talk."

The girl looked the other way, and he followed me back behind the dumpster.

I looked into his eyes, and his gaze was ice cold. I glanced at the lips I had kissed a thousand times. They were pressed into a thin line. This was the person I'd dated for three years, but neither of us had been happy together. We had a love-hate relationship. We hated the way we treated each other, so we broke up. But we loved getting back together. This time I knew "back together" wouldn't happen. Not after the decision I was making.

"I'm pregnant," I told him flat out.

His expression didn't change. "I don't believe you."

My hands protectively covered my stomach. I raised my voice. "Fine, don't believe me. I don't need you anyway. This baby doesn't need you."

That was one of the last times I talked to him. Ever.

One day I was a typical high school senior. An honors student, a cheerleader, and a yearbook editor. I worked part-time at McDonald's to pay for gas and clothes.

The next day, I was a mother-to-be. I knew lots of people who had babies, even a few at my school. But what would it mean for me?

One thing I knew for sure: I wanted to have this baby. After the abortion, something inside me shut down. I couldn't deal with my emotions, so I flipped them off like a light switch. I hated myself for deciding to put my life ahead of my child's.

The second time around, I dealt with my pregnancy by hiding from the world. I stopped going to school because I hated people staring at me, talking about me. I hated seeing my boyfriend with his new girlfriend. I dropped out of regular high school and attended a community school for troubled teens. I even quit my part-time job at McDonald's because the smell of the food cooking made me sick.

Within a couple of months, my life nauseated me. I went nowhere, did nothing. My friends continued with their senior year. And my baby's daddy was out of the picture.

I was my own worst enemy. I was lonely and scared. Grumpy and standoffish. I felt like a kid, but now I had a huge responsibility. How could I be a mother?

Yet even though my life seemed out of control in so many ways, I was happy about one thing: I was excited to be a mom. I was excited to have a baby. I didn't know much about life, but even when I found out I was pregnant, I was looking forward to having a child.

A boy? A girl? It didn't matter. I was going to be a mom.

What about You?

What did you do when you found out you were pregnant? The most common reaction is panic and worry. Maybe it's a complete surprise. Maybe you sort of expected it. After spending time with teen moms over the last twelve years, I've heard many stories.

- Some moms discovered they were having twins. *(Did you have any surprises?)*
- Some moms got unusual requests from parents, like, "Can I have your baby?" *(What would you have said?)*
- Some baby daddies were excited. Others were mad. Some were gone—out of the picture. Others were committed. *(How did your baby daddy respond?)*
- Some moms knew right away they would have their babies. Others questioned whether they should just get an abortion. *(Did you struggle with the decision to become a mom?)*

Many stories are similar to Haven's:[1] "I got a pregnancy test and then stopped at the nearest gas station to take it. In a cold, dirty bathroom, I found out a baby was coming … What had I gotten myself into? How was I going to tell my mom?"

Another young woman, Kendra,[2] found out she was pregnant when she went into the emergency room and discovered she was in labor. Talk about the shock of your life!

Then there are those who are happy about being pregnant, like

Kayleigh. When she was only fifteen, she wanted to have a baby. For most of her life, Kayleigh had been sexually abused. Her innocence had been taken away, and she wanted to get away from the situation. She thought expecting a baby would solve everything. She and her boyfriend could get their own place, and they could start their own family. So she was thrilled to discover she was pregnant.

No matter how you found out, no matter what others thought about your pregnancy, there is one thing that all of us have in common—our lives changed. We had to think of someone other than ourselves. We had to learn how to deal with all the changes. We lost friends, and sadly, we were seen by many as simply a statistic.

Everyone has an opinion about teen pregnancy. Some people see it as a problem. Some see it as an obstacle or a hinderance to teens' future. Shows like MTV's *Teen Mom* give people a glimpse into teen pregnancy, but *their story is not ours*. You are not a statistic. Your child is not a statistic. Your future has just as many possibilities the day after you discover that you are a pregnant teen as it did the day before.

I'll be the first to tell you that life will be harder. There are more challenges. But your life can be just as good.

Things Change

When you find out you're pregnant, things change. Maybe your parents are angry; maybe they're excited. Maybe your boyfriend is excited. Maybe he's angry. Some teen moms stay in school and work hard to do their best, but others decide that they can't handle one more thing and drop out of school. Some teens get support from their parents. Others get kicked out of their homes.

One of my friends, Jamie, had already broken up with her boyfriend by the time she found out she was pregnant. Scared, she didn't tell her mom for three months.

"I knew my mom would be disappointed," Jamie told me. "And she was. But my dad was worse. He didn't talk to me for almost my whole pregnancy. Not a phone call, nothing."

Then we have to deal with being responsible for a new life. "The thing that keeps me up at night is the idea that I'm a mother," Jamie confessed. "I just can't believe it."

Things change once you discover you're pregnant. They change even more when you become a mom. Some changes are wonderful. Some are painful and dramatic. Here are a few stats so you know you're not alone:

- In 2012, there were 29.4 births for every one thousand adolescent females ages fifteen to nineteen, or 305,388 babies born to females in this age group. Nearly 89 percent of these births occurred outside of marriage.[3]
- The 2012 teen birth rate indicates a decline of 6 percent from 2011, when the birth rate was 31.3 per thousand.[4]
- Estimates from 2010 data show that one in seven adolescent females (14.4 percent) in the United States will give birth by her twentieth birthday, with substantial differences by race or ethnicity: 10 percent of white adolescent females, 21 percent of black adolescent females, and 24 percent of Hispanic adolescent females.[5] The number of babies born to women ages fifteen to nineteen was 367,752 in 2010 (the most recent count).[6]

My Life

"I was riding around in my mom's little convertible and I had not been feeling well. I thought it was just stress with work and all kinds of different things. My friend was like, 'Why don't you just take a test?' I was like, 'Okay, I will.' We were filling up with gas, so I went in the gas station and took the test and it was positive," she recalls. "So that is the glamorous way that I found out I was going to have my little nugget!"

— Jamie Lynn Spears

You are one of that 367,752, but like I said, you are more than a statistic! You are a person with hopes and dreams, with fears and needs. And so is every one of the 367,751 other moms.

You're not alone. Many others are facing the same things. Life changes for every young person; for some it changes a bit more when they become a parent. While there may not be anything glamorous about these changes, you can find help and hope. Mom, you are stronger than you think.

What Do You Need?

I've been leading a support group for teen moms for the last twelve years. Every Thursday night, I hang out with pregnant and parenting young women. I've led support groups in Montana and in Arkansas. I've met teen moms all around the US. No two moms look alike or have the same walk in life. Each one has a different story, but they all have needs. They need friendship. They need love. They need help and support. They need parenting tips. They need to know they matter.

In my groups, there have been moms from middle-class families. They have their own cars and sometimes apartments. These young moms often feel like they're the "black sheep" of the family. They were the ones who tainted their family's perfect image, and they hear about it all the time.

There are also moms who are very familiar with teen pregnancy. Their moms were teen moms. Their aunties were teen moms. Their grandmothers were teen moms. It's not a surprise when they become teen moms too.

Whether teen pregnancy is unique to your family or it's common, whether you are from a middle-class family or your family struggles to get by, teen moms have similar needs. Teen moms all over have the same struggles, worries, and concerns. We also have the same joys and triumphs. We share many things in common, and we will be discussing these various topics throughout this book.

At the end of each chapter are activities that you can do to help you think through what you learned. Do them by yourself or find a friend to do them with you. Mostly, do them! These activities will help you in your role as a mom.

Back to My Motherhood Story

I gave birth to my son three weeks after my high school graduation. If you think those graduation gowns are unfashionable, imagine how they'd look on someone eight months pregnant!

I'm writing this book as someone who's been there. Someone who has felt the stares of a condemning world. Someone who dropped out of high school and graduated through alternative education. Someone who had to face the heartbreak of seeing him with her—the beautiful, not-pregnant, new girlfriend.

I'm also writing as one who has found success and joy in the years after teen parenting. I married a wonderful man, had two more kids, adopted three more after that, and embarked on a successful writing career. That's in addition to leading teen mom support groups!

But the road between there and here wasn't easy. I wish my story played out like a children's book: The pregnant princess meets Prince Charming. Then she marries him and goes to live in his castle. They live happily ever after. The end. Instead, my story is like a novel full of troubles and triumphs, both of which I'll share with you.

My goal for this book is to encourage you by sharing my story and the stories of other young moms. I also want to provide advice that I would have appreciated when I was a new mother at seventeen.

Friend, I want you to know that I believe in you. I believe that you can be a good mom and have a good life. Your story may have a bump in the road, but today is the day when everything can change. Everything can start moving in the right direction. I won't tell you that life will be easy. It won't. It never is. But I will tell you that life can be good—for you. And for your child. You're reading this book, aren't you? You've already made a wonderful first step!

Finding out you were pregnant was a life-changing event, but today can be one too. Just open your mind and heart to the good future that's available to you. Do it for yourself, for your child.

1

Do I Matter?

Importance

*The deepest principle in the human nature is the craving to be
appreciated.*

— William James, author

I regretted attending the basketball game as soon as I got there. My
classmates, teachers, and friends' parents cheered on our school's
basketball team. I moved to the bleachers closest to the door and
climbed to the top row, sitting next to some of my friends.

My jeans pinched my stomach as I sat. They were the biggest
pair I had, and at five months pregnant, I'd barely been able to button
them up. Now they cut into my gut, but I tried to ignore the pinching
feeling. I tried to ignore how my body was changing and how I had
no control of it. I also tried to ignore the glances as people eyed me.
Could they see the baby bump that I was trying so hard to hide?

After finding out I was pregnant, everything changed. I felt so
sick that even on days when I attended school, I usually went home
early. Soon it was easier just to stay home altogether. I couldn't work
either. Every whiff of fast-food smell made me nauseated.

And then there was the *growing*. My stomach, my chest, my …
everything. I had taken pride in being able to wear a tiny cheerleading skirt, but now my body no longer felt like it was mine.

Overnight, my lifestyle changed too. Intead of eating cheeseburgers and fries numerous times a week, I had to make sure I drank enough water, took my prenatal vitamins, and ate healthy foods. I tried to get enough sleep and not stress too much about my life. (Yeah, right.)

I had to go to the doctor and get weighed and measured every month, and I submitted to being "checked" in ways that creeped me out. And I didn't even want to think about labor. It was like knowing ahead of time that you were going to get in a car accident or break your arm, and counting down the days.

Of course, the physical discomfort and the numerous changes and fears were nothing compared with the ache in my soul. It felt like someone had stuck a knife in my heart as I watched my old cheerleading squad do the routines that I'd known so well. Another cheerleader had taken my spot once I'd left the squad, and it didn't feel good to be replaced.

Even worse was seeing my baby's daddy sitting a few rows down with his new girlfriend. I'd been replaced there too. He was going on with his life as if nothing had changed. He'd chosen to walk away from responsibility, and so for him nothing *had* changed. For me everything was different. We'd made a baby together, but I was the one paying the price.

I sat through part of the game, but I wasn't really watching it. More than anything, I wanted to hide, to run. I didn't feel as if I fit in here anymore. I'd gone to school with the same group of students since kindergarten, and I felt like an outsider among them. They didn't know what to say to me, and the things they seemed so obsessed about seemed silly to me now. I was going to be a mom. Talking about clothes and whose house the party was going to be at didn't matter to me anymore.

Of course, I didn't fit in at home either. My parents did their best to be supportive, but I discovered that I had to make so many decisions myself, like how to finish school and what I was going to do after my baby was born. I was still a kid in their house, and at times they liked to treat me as one, but I was also making so many big decisions. Was I just fooling myself thinking I could handle all of this?

It wasn't just me I had to think about. After my prenatal visit, the nurse had sent me home with brochures on things I should be eating. There were vitamins I was supposed to take, but they were hard to remember. Worries plagued me too. What if I did something and hurt the baby inside me? I'd never be able to forgive myself.

> In this life we cannot always do great things. But we can do small things with great love.
>
> —*Mother Teresa*

I left the basketball game early, during halftime, and the drive home seemed to take longer than normal. I knew that no one really cared that I'd left early. Maybe it was easier for them when I wasn't there—then they didn't have to worry about what to say or what to do.

The moon hung overhead as I drove, and I'd never felt so alone and so unimportant.

Could I do it? This mom thing? Or was I just a kid trying to act like an adult, fooling no one except myself?

My Life

Some people have given me dirty looks when they see me with my baby. Others look at me and sigh. But some people are very nice when they see what a good mom I am.

—*Diana, Washington*

Life Interrupted

These were supposed to be years of parties, football games, and fun. Dances with handsome dates and sleepovers with friends. You've gone from chatting with friends in the hall to changing dirty diapers. Not long ago the only runny nose you wiped was your own. Colic wasn't an issue. Your clothes were spit-up free. Now you wonder where your importance is.

When your baby came into the picture, you not only lost your old life but gained a new one. Many of us know, without a doubt, that having our babies was the right choice. We want to be good moms. We want to give our babies the love that we, perhaps, never had. But if we're honest, we can't help but think how our lives have changed. Sometimes we wonder whether it's worth it.

My Life

When I found out I was pregnant, I was incredibly scared and didn't know how to tell my parents. They'd always said they'd kill me if I ever ended up pregnant.

—Desiree, *Texas*

Before my pregnancy, I was in four clubs and had a meeting almost every night. Most of my friends have completely left the picture. I figured they would, but I feel very alone. Having a baby has really helped me to see who my real friends are.

— Amanda, *Ontario, Canada*

Tell Me I'm Important

Young moms want to be good moms. We try our best; we really do. Yet we can't seem to escape the negative reactions. We've decided to carry and keep our babies. (Not an easy decision!) But often the people we encounter make it clear, both in words and with body language, that they disapprove. Sometimes we feel we have no importance.

What you do is important. Can you think of anyone who loves your child more than you do? You're the exact person your child needs to love him, support him, and be his biggest fan.

For the rest of your life, when your child hears the word *mother*, he will think of *you*. You are the first one to tell him of his importance, to believe in his dreams, and to kiss his boo-boos, wishing his hurts away.

Your child doesn't realize that you're young. He has *no* idea. To him you are the most perfect mom in the world. Yes, you!

You Are Important

Importance means having meaning. There are many things that people feel are important for young people: school, good grades, sports, and accomplishments.

Ask yourself, What things were important to you one or two years ago? What things are important now?

Your child, no doubt, is most important. And your child thinks *you* are most important. Without your succeeding as a mom, his life is going to be hard.

The good news is that you're up to the task. This mothering role will teach you more about yourself than you ever expected. You'll work harder than you ever have. You'll prove you're strong and capable. Your care for your child will not only benefit him, but it'll also show you (and the world!) what you're made of.

Parenting comes with big obstacles at times. Yet as you'll see in the following often-told story, sometimes human beings can do the impossible when it comes to their children.

Moving Mountains

"There were two warring tribes in the Andes, one that lived in the lowlands and the other high in the mountains. The mountain people invaded the lowlanders one day, and as part of their plundering of the people, they kidnapped a baby from one of the lowlander families and took the infant back with them up into the mountains.

"The lowlanders didn't know how to climb a mountain. They didn't know any of the trails the mountain people used, and they didn't know where to find the mountain people or how to track them on the steep terrain.

"Even so, they sent out their best party of fighting men to climb the mountain and bring the baby home.

"The men tried first one method of climbing and then another. They tried one trail and then another. After several days of effort, however, they had climbed only a couple of hundred feet.

"Feeling hopeless and helpless, the lowlander men decided that the case was lost, and they prepared to return to their village below.

"As they were packing their gear for the descent, they saw the baby's mother walking toward them. They realized that she was coming down the mountain that they hadn't figured out how to climb.

"And then they saw that she had the baby strapped to her back. How could that be?

"One man greeted her and said, 'We couldn't climb this mountain. How did you do this when we, the strongest and most able men in the village, couldn't do it?'

"She shrugged her shoulders and said, 'It wasn't your baby.' "[1]

You're a mom now, and the obstacles you face may seem as big and insurmountable as that mountain. But there's one thing that's even more powerful than your challenges. That's your love. Love is the most important ingredient when it comes to parenting. Love, as you will discover, can help you to achieve the impossible.

Before getting pregnant, I hadn't thought much about what I wanted to do with my life, except that I'd considered being a teacher and hoped to be married with three or four kids someday. After getting pregnant, I thought it really was no use to think about those things anymore because I had messed up. I was going to have a baby, and so I'd just have to take whatever the world offered me from there.

Do you feel that way? Do you think that because you're a mom at a young age that all the plans you once had aren't possible? Maybe you never really considered what your future looked like. Maybe you never allowed yourself to dream. I want to encourage you to get over the idea that because you're having a baby at a young age, you can't do much with your life. Instead, you now have an even better reason to dream and plan for a good future. After all, you have not only yourself to think about but also your child.

It would have been easy for me to just give up and not try. I'd seen that time and time again in the people around me. I have many family members who've worked minimum wage jobs their whole lives, who have never owned a home, and who never got their high school diploma. In fact, when I found out I was pregnant, I dropped out of high school too.

I'm thankful that I dared to work hard to achieve my goals. I finished my high school classes at home and got my diploma. Here are a few other things I've done:

- I've attended college.
- I've gotten married.
- I've attended numerous writers' conferences.
- I've written hundreds of articles for national magazines.
- I've won awards for my writing.
- I've written more than forty-five books.
- I've homeschooled three children all the way from kindergarten through high school.
- I've traveled to more than forty states.
- I've traveled to twelve countries.
- I've been interviewed on television.
- I've hosted my own radio show.
- I've been married for twenty-five years.
- I've adopted three kids.
- My husband and I have bought three houses. (One at a time!)
- I've helped start a crisis pregnancy center.
- I've led a teen moms' support group for twelve years.
- I've shared my story of being a teenage mom on stage in front of five thousand women.
- I've taken my kids to Disneyland and Disney World many times, and my whole family has gone on a cruise.

I'm forty-three years old, which may seem ancient to you, but I've had a good life. And I didn't do all those things right away, but as the years have gone by, I've been amazed to see how my life has turned out.

When I first had my son, I wondered whether my life would amount to anything, and then I decided it could if I put in some effort. My goals were small at first. I got my high school diploma, and then I signed up for college classes. I went on a date with a really good guy who treated me well, and we eventually got married. I dreamed of becoming a writer, and so I babysat for a year to save up enough money to attend my first writers' conference.

At that writers' conference, I met other women who encouraged me, and I kept in touch with them. I wrote little things while my kids napped. (I had three kids by this time.) And I sent things out to magazines. I got more than a hundred rejections, but I didn't give up. I saved up my money again and went back to the conference. Soon I started getting magazine articles published, and later, books.

Success has a way of building on itself. Hard work pays off eventually. If you could be successful at anything, what would it be? Consider one step that you could take toward that dream. Every success starts with a first step.

Think you can't do it? Think that you'll be stuck where you are forever? It's up to you. You get to decide!

The years are going to go by anyway, and you might as well spend them pursuing something great. You can either spend your teens and twenties working at McDonald's with no plan to change, or you can work hard at your McDonald's job, finish your GED, sign up for college, and get an internship at a job you really love.

No, there's nothing wrong with working at McDonald's, but is that how you want to spend your life? I thought about this when I returned to northern California for a high school reunion. I took my kids to McDonald's to show them where I once worked. Twenty years had passed and the building looked tired and old, but I was most surprised when I saw that some of the people I had worked with in high school were still there. They were still complaining about their jobs and about how they still weren't able to make ends meet, but they hadn't done anything about it.

It's wonderful to work wherever you can get a job, but don't limit yourself. I saw my McDonald's job as a stepping-stone to get the money I needed to do more. Who knows, maybe you'll even stay with McDonald's, work your way through management, and buy a franchise! Just remember that you're stronger than you think. Don't give up too easily. Don't settle when, deep down, you know you can do more, give more.

My Life

I get so tired of people asking, "How old are you?" We even had to change pediatricians once because the doctor wouldn't speak to me as an adult. I wanted to yell, "Hey, I am her mother. I'm responsible for her welfare!" I used to cry at night, not because I didn't want this but because I had no idea how much my life would change.

— Marjie, Montana

When I went into the hospital for my non-stress test, the nurse told me that she wanted my baby and that she would prepare the adoption papers if it was a boy.

— Amanda, Ontario, Canada

Waking up to my son's smile and my daughter's snoring makes me realize that the little things these little people do will forever be engraved in my heart!

— Elizabeth, Arkansas

Mom, you're the one who will determine your future. Don't let anyone tell you that you can't amount to anything. That's not true. You can work hard to achieve anything you set your mind on.

Surround yourself with people who believe in you. Find other people who can support you, help you, and offer help in return.

Also, know that you were created for a reason. God made you, formed you. He made and formed your child. He has a good plan for your life. You are important to God, and that makes you important.

And even if you don't "accomplish" anything that makes the news, you are still important to God. You are also still important to your child.

But sometimes understanding that you *are* important helps you to go on to do great things. Think of it this way, if you tell your child day after day that he is going to do great things and help and influence people, he will most likely grow up to do great things and help and influence people. And if you say the same thing about yourself, well, that's exactly what you will do too.

The Balancing Act

Just because a mom is willing to do anything for her child doesn't mean it's easy. Motherhood can be illustrated by an image of a woman wearing a tower of hats. There is the nurse's hat, the teacher's hat, the maid's hat, the cook's hat, the playmate's hat—the list goes on. As a young mom, your problem may be the many hats you haven't discarded: the student's hat, the employee's hat, the girlfriend's hat, even the daughter-at-home's hat. How can you—one person—balance so much responsibility?

Your balancing act will change over time. The hat of high school student may change to that of college student. The playground-mom's hat may change to the soccer mom's. Still, the flow of your responsibilities will never end.

The reality of being a mom may not hit until you come home from the hospital. The feedings, the diapers, the schedule, the up-all-nights. Then, as one stage passes, there are more challenges: teething, climbing on everything, tantrums, and on and on.

Of course, there's a sweet part of the reality too. The smiles, the soft snores. The cuddles and the coos!

The worst part is doing it alone. Some young moms have a baby daddy who has stuck around. Perhaps your family helps. Friends may come around now and then. But there are always days when it feels like it's you and this kid against the world.

You will need to balance your emotions along with all your responsibilities. When you start feeling down, *you're* the one who will need to remind yourself that you're important, no matter how hard it is.

In addition to feeling overwhelmed, you will also need to deal with those things called hormones. There were days when I was pregnant that I couldn't stop crying. The same happened postpartum, after my baby was born. It helped when a friend told me that the hormones raging through my body had a lot to do with that. I've had friends who have even sunk into deep depression and needed medication to help balance them out. This isn't something to be ashamed of. Instead, it's a great reminder that things are often better than our emotions tell us they are. In fact, I've discovered it helps to remind myself that.

Sometimes you'll tell yourself, "Things will be better tomorrow," when you're rolling up your sleeves to dive into a task. And other times you'll tell yourself, "I'm important, no matter how I'm feeling," and you realize this is true when your child cries and you're the only one who can bring him comfort. Both actions and positive thoughts are a good way to combat the negative thoughts. Both are needed. Just remember to tell yourself of your importance often. And notice that same importance in your child's eyes.

Stereotyped by Society

It's hard being a good mom and worse when people judge you because of your age. As if they think you sleep with just anyone. They assume you're doomed to fail. Sometimes they see that you come from the "bad part of town" and they assume you won't amount to anything. It's hard to live with stereotypes, and as long as you live, you will face them. But the best part is that God doesn't do stereotypes. In fact, he likes to use the least likely people to do amazing things. For example, in the Bible we can read about a young shepherd boy named David whom God chose to be king over Israel. Or, my favorite, God chose an unmarried teenager to become the mother of his Son—oh yes he did! It's almost like he enjoys proving the world wrong.

We all, at times, worry what others think. I remember the first time I stood in line at the welfare office. I needed help with medical costs, food, living expenses—you name it. But before going, I made sure I looked my best (which some people might have judged too!). I didn't want to be stereotyped as someone who was uneducated and unmotivated. I wanted others to respect me, despite the situation I was in.

And, yes, I did live on government assistance for a time. I needed it to get by. I needed help to provide for my baby, and there is no shame in doing so. But I didn't let myself get accustomed to it. Instead, I worked really hard to make myself better. I still give 100 percent to all the tasks I'm given. Sometimes people notice. Other times they don't. Whether people notice doesn't matter as much as my doing the best job I can.

This hard work has been good for me. And it's good for my children to see. By working hard, I've broken free of the stereotypes, and that feels good. People no longer judge me for being a young mom. It's just one part of my story. Being a young mom made me grow up and change. It turned me toward God. It caused me to work hard because I had another person depending on me. I've proven that a young mom can go on to do amazing things. You can too!

Don't Give Up

When I faced the reality of being a young mother, I could have given up. I could have accepted that many young moms never graduate from high school and live in poverty for the rest of their lives. But inside, I knew I wasn't someone the world could write off. I simply had found myself in way over my head. I was a smart young woman who would love my child completely.

Because of this, I decided to believe in myself and to take the distasteful looks in stride. I strove to be an antistereotype and show the world what a young mom can accomplish.

Ponderings from a Young Mom

Is there a magical age that makes mothering okay? Can I hold my head high at twenty? Twenty-five? Thirty? What makes a good mom? A nice paycheck? A house in the suburbs? Will people respect me if I enroll my child in a private preschool? Or dress him in designer clothes?

Or is it enough just to love him? To read stories at bedtime? To kiss baby toes and tickle baby bellies? To smile? To dream? It may not be enough for society. But it will be enough for me. For my child.

I will not let the world tell me an age that motherhood is okay. Instead, I will become the mother my child needs, and find joy in the simple moments as I do it.

I realized my importance came from within me. I couldn't please everyone all the time. I couldn't change my situation overnight, but I could take steps to improve. I could work at becoming a great mom. And it worked!

As I believed in myself and trusted in my importance as a mother, my confidence grew. Like a small snowball kicked down a steep hill, I picked up speed and grew as a person. Soon I became unstoppable!

How about you? Do you feel you need to please others? Instead simply consider how you can make yourself the best you possible.

Don't give up. Don't let the beliefs of others hinder the changes that you can make happen. Every day think of one thing you can do to improve yourself, and ask God to help you make that change.

You will change. You will grow. You will become unstoppable!

Home Life: the Bad, the Good, and the Missing

Have you noticed that the only people who truly welcome change are wet babies?

— Anonymous

The Bad

It's hard enough that "the world" looks down on you. But what if you face negative attitudes at home? Many young moms who still live with their parents may feel like the cream in the middle of an Oreo. They're sandwiched between their parents and their child. Only this situation is not sweet. These young moms are parents, but they still live by their parents' rules. These moms get advice from all directions and may feel like they're "mothering by committee."

I hear it all the time from the young moms I know. Since they are still living at home, their mothers want to make all the rules — to tell them how to dress their kids and what to feed them. Sometimes these young moms feel they've been left out of the decision making.

If this is your case, try to see your parents' point of view, but also get them to understand yours. It's key that you realize your importance as a mother. Once you accept that and take responsibility in your new role, hopefully your parents will realize your importance too.

Of course, sometimes the negative attitudes are for a reason. I know teen moms who have a baby and who expect their parents to do all the work. They get mad when their parents don't babysit and won't give them spending money. Don't be this kind of mom. Remember, it's your child and your responsibility. If you act responsibly, your parents should respect that. Don't believe it? Try it and give your parents a chance. And even if your parents aren't willing to commend your efforts, you'll be a better person when you're responsible. And your child will have a wonderful example to follow.

34

The Good

For others, becoming a young parent can strengthen family bonds. This was true in my case. Right away my "friends" ditched me. But my family stayed and cared. They stuck by me and believed in me.

My parents and grandparents helped me to realize my importance, even on days when I wanted to sleep in and hide from the world. They helped by letting me make my own parenting decisions. And I soon learned my decisions mattered.

I couldn't have done what I've done without the help of my mom. She was there to show me how to give Cory a bath. There were times she'd rock him in the night when Cory had colic. For so many years, I'd pushed my mom away as I spent time with my boyfriends and wanted to do things with friends. When I realized I needed my mom, she was there for me, and I was thankful.

Good came from the challenge of being a teen mom. My son was one good thing. My growing relationship with my mom was another.

How about you? Can you find a way to build bonds with your parents now that you've become a parent yourself?

As you build bonds with your parents, you create invaluable connections for your child with his grandparents. You help to nurture and build that relationship as well.

It's a hard world out there; children need as much love poured into them as possible. We can help that along. No family is perfect. No one's parents are perfect, but we can focus on the good. Grandparents can help to love and support both you and your child when given the chance.

The Missing

So far I've mentioned the type of parents who want to take over your role. I've also talked about the parents who step up and really help. There is another type of parent: "the missing parent."

Missing can mean so many things. I know a number of teen moms whose mothers have passed away. Some of them have moms in jail. Others have been abandoned by their moms or have been taken from their mothers' care and put into the foster care system. And there are those who were kicked out when they became pregnant.

Then there are those whose mothers are around, but it's not a healthy relationship. A positive role model is missing in this case.

No matter what our age, we understand our mothers better when we become moms. As my friend Amy told me, "We're able, for the first time, to walk in our mothers' shoes. And we realize how much we need them. The mom role is so overwhelming. It's a gift to have a mom who is willing to come alongside and just be there, or offer practical advice, or simply let us still be daughters and not have to be in mom mode all the time. But sometimes, we have moms who are just not available. But the need for them does not go away."

Do you have a need like this? Do you wish you had a mother who cares, who can love you unconditionally, or who is there for you—whether physically or emotionally?

Everyone needs a mother figure to look up to. If your mother isn't around, consider who could step into the role. Is there a neighbor, a coworker, or an older woman at church you can turn to for advice? Go to her. Ask for prayer or encouragement. Let her know that you appreciate her insights.

Many older moms don't feel they have a lot to offer. They are often more focused on their parenting failures than their successes. Letting an older mom know that you appreciate her influence in your life will make a difference. Not only for yourself but for her too.

Looking up to someone reminds them of their importance, and having a caring influence in your life will remind you of yours.

My Life

My mother constantly says, "I love you and the baby, but I wish you had waited until you were done with school." My friends have said, "You're amazing! I can't imagine doing this!" They also say, "I wouldn't want to have a baby right now." Some comments are positive, and others not.

— Amanda, *Ontario, Canada*

Your God-Given Role

Faced with work and school responsibilities, most young moms don't have the luxury of staying home with their children. But even if your child is in the daily care of someone else for one hour or ten hours, you're still the mom.

Although you can never list "good mother" on a job resume, this role should not be diminished. Mothering isn't rewarded with a big paycheck or your name on the dean's list, but you're the only mother your child will have. Or as author Kate Douglas Wiggin puts it, "Most of all the other beautiful things in life come by twos and threes, by dozens and hundreds. Plenty of roses, stars, sunsets, rainbows, brothers and sisters, aunts and cousins, but only one mother in the whole world."

God chose you to be that "one mother in the whole world" for your child. And if that doesn't show your importance, I don't know what does.

You were chosen to be this child's mom for a reason. And while others can see only your exterior, God has a unique ability to see the heart. He can also see your potential to be a great mom.

Take a moment to think of God. Consider the role he has chosen for you to be your baby's mom. How does it make you feel to know that he trusts you with this child? What do you want to do, knowing that trust?

Positive Parenting

Another reason why your role is important is because the better mother you become, the better person your child will be for life.

As you may know, the first three years of a child's life are critical for the learning process. According to the American Academy of Pediatrics, "The ways in which parents interact with their children will set the stage for an infant's growth and development for life."

This is the time when you, as a mom, play a huge part in deciding who your child will be. Here are just a few key areas.

> "Dance with your children, be silly with them, make mistakes and allow yourself to be human occasionally. They'll love you for it."
>
> — *Anne Geddes*, A Labor of Love

- The food you provide helps your child's body to grow strong.
- Your hugs, kisses, and kind words build your child's sense of worth.
- Your love shows him the importance of loving others.
- Interactive play shapes his physical and mental abilities.

What you provide during these early years is the foundation a life is built upon. Just as a skyscraper needs concrete and steel for stability, your child needs solid love and steadfast commitment.

To be a good mother, you don't need a nice car, a huge house, or a successful career. You don't need access to expensive toys. What's needed most is you.

"Mothering isn't about tasks," says author Cheri Fuller. "It's about building a relationship that lasts a lifetime."

What you do today will last a lifetime!

My Life

Having a baby pretty much grounded me. Before I had a baby, I guess you could say I was a wild teen. I was rude, inconsiderate, not caring about anything. But when I had a baby, I realized I was going to have to grow up really fast. I needed to set an example.

— Diana, *Washington*

Final Thoughts

Becoming a mother has helped many young moms consider what they want from life. It's helped them get on track.

It definitely helped me to get on track. Once I became pregnant, I realized that my plans for a good future were not only vital for me, but they were also important for my child. My thought process changed. I now wondered what I should do about schooling. What classes could I take at the community college to help me in a future career? What job would I enjoy that would still allow me to spend quality time with my son?

Right now, your major decisions may center on your schooling options. Or they may be about where you should work or live. No matter what choices you're facing, mothering provides an opportunity to become a better person. A better person for yourself. For your future. For your child.

Overcoming Overwhelming Emotions

Know yourself and what will help you on overwhelming days. Sometimes as young moms we get so busy doing things that we forget to touch base with our emotions. For example, I've learned that when I'm overwhelmed, it usually means I'm hungry or tired. If I'm hungry, I eat something healthy. If I'm tired, I take a nap. When I'm angry, I often need time to get away and pray. Knowing what you need helps you to combat emotions that tell you that you're not important.

Read the following list and circle any of the feelings you've experienced. When you're finished, consider who or what has helped you overcome these feelings. Then consider how you can overcome these feelings the next time they arise.

angry	inexperienced	overwhelmed
doubtful	unaccepted	trapped
scared	anxious	unimportant
nervous	uncertain	unappreciated
incapable	inadequate	alone

Attitude Adjustment

Moving beyond Stereotypes

An attitude adjustment begins with you. Take a minute to quickly list some negative things you've heard, read, or thought about young parents. Across from each negative statement, write two positive statements to reflect your experience. Here's an example. Try to come up with three more.

Stereotype	Reality
Young moms are too immature to raise a child.	Young parents have energy and know how to have fun!

Speaking Meaningful Words

Messages for Baby

Check out the messages your baby needs most. Remember to tell your child often how important he is.

- *"I belong."* Those hours in your arms give your baby the message, "I am loved. Somebody's there for me."
- *"I'm special."* It is never too early to begin affirming your baby and letting him know how valuable he is in God's eyes and in your heart.
- *"I trust."* Because in his distress you comfort him, your baby learns that you will respond and are worthy of his trust.
- *"I can."* Applaud your baby's milestones. Show your joy as he stretches his little body and his mind.[2]

Do I Matter?

Here's your assignment: Look at yourself in the mirror and tell yourself the same things you just told your baby. Finish these sentences:

- "I belong because ..."
- "I'm special because ..."
- "I trust when ..."
- "I can ..."

How Mothering Has Changed Everything

We could go on all day about the importance of mothering in the life of a child, but have you considered how mothering has affected you? Take a few minutes to write down your thoughts.

Live and Learn

My love today will mold my child's tomorrows!

2

Who Am I?

Identity

People always say how you should be yourself, like yourself is this definite thing, like a toaster or something.

— Angela, *My So-Called Life*

I remember my first day of junior college like it was yesterday. I lived in a small town, and my high school graduating class was around forty people. I'd gone to school with most of the same people from kindergarten through high school, and even though I stopped going to high school classes, the principal signed me up for a program that allowed me to finish my last credits from home. As I walked into my first class at college, I looked around and saw many of the same faces.

The last time I had seen most of these people was at our high school graduation. We'd all been wearing caps and gowns, and my gown had stuck out farther than the rest with a baby bump. Graduation had been just three weeks before my due date. My face was puffy and my ankles were swollen. While they'd been talking about summer vacation, part-time jobs, and road trips, I was considering baby names and birth.

Their lives hadn't changed much from high school to college, but my life was completely different. I had to think about babysitting, and I did my homework with a baby on my lap. They were dating people who liked to drink and party, and I was wondering whether there was a guy out there who could open his heart to me and to my son.

I remember once when my babysitting fell through, and I stopped by my math class to drop off my homework. I walked in with the car seat in one hand and my homework in the other. My baby was sleeping and the professor told me I could stay. Of course Cory woke up during the class and distracted everyone. As I pulled him out of his car seat, his chubby hands reached for my pencil, and then he almost poked himself in the eye.

After class my friends wanted to hold him, and when we finally walked away, I realized I had no idea who I was anymore. I still felt like them—young, wanting to have fun, trying to do good enough in college, and having big dreams.

But the other part of me was responsible for a child. I knew how challenging it was when a babysitter backed out at the last minute. I knew that one little being could change a day's plans when he was teething or when he had a tummy ache. I couldn't just think of myself anymore. I had to make plans—not just about the weekend but also about our future.

In high school I used to know who I was. I was a good student, a cheerleader, and a kid who didn't get in much trouble, but I was still trying to figure out who I was as a mom. My body was different, and I sometimes had spit-up on my shirt. I couldn't stay up too late or sleep in. I didn't hang out with my friends because I couldn't relate to them. While caring for a baby, I didn't have the time to hang out with friends. Yet I really couldn't relate to older moms either.

Who have I become? I asked myself more than once as I tried to do complex math problems then cooed over my baby boy the next moment. I was a student and a daughter, although those roles had changed dramatically. I was an employee too, working part-time at the college to help cover my tuition. And I was a mom. More than anything, that last role had overshadowed all the others, leaving little room for anything else.

While I wouldn't have traded my son for the world, I wondered, *Who am I? Is there any "me" left?*

My Life

I'm learning by doing things as a mum, and I grow every time I do something for my son. It's hard to find my identity. Sometimes I don't feel like I'm growing up and other times I do.

— Sarah, *Australia*

My life has changed so much since having my daughter. I can't do the things that I used to. I don't have half the friends I did before. I'm having to grow up faster than I should.

— Nina, *Texas*

I'm Not Sure Who I Am

All of us moms—whether we've been a mom for a few days or a few years—ask ourselves the same question. "Who am I?" When our children enter the world, they not only have their own identity, but they take ours as well. Suddenly we're not in charge of our lives. We're not even in charge of our minutes. We become diaper-changing, baby-feeding, baby-rocking, nonsense-cooing mamas.

But even though we've become moms, we're still the same people. We like to hang out with friends. We want to sleep in, and we want to dress in cute clothes. Young moms I know like to get their hair done, their nails done, and they have an idea for their next tattoo. Just because they've had a baby doesn't mean everything's changed.

The problem is that to be responsible moms, we can't hang out with our friends like we used to. We can't stay out all night and sleep all day. At first our friends seem to understand, but soon it's too hard for them to try to work around our schedules. We often find ourselves friendless, fun-less, unavailable, and broke.

Think about It

The day your baby is born you begin to discover who this new person is. In your child, a new identity is born. But on that day a second person is also born: a mom. Whether you like it or not, you're a different person from the one who began the labor process.

In what ways are you different after becoming a mom?

Your Identity

As new mothers we often need help defining who we are. Does who we are depend on what we do? Does it depend on how we look, or what others think about us? The answer is no. Who we are goes deeper than that. It's our inner self that only we know. But discovering our identity isn't a concern only for young moms. Mothers of all ages and in all stages ask the same questions.

After the birth of her child, a mom moves from focusing on her personal needs to being driven by the needs of a small human being. And although she may enjoy her new role (most of the time), there are days when she looks in the mirror, sees a stranger, and asks, *Who are you?*

Identity is a strange balance of understanding your likes, dislikes, and temperament, yet balancing that with your roles as daughter, student, employee, and mom. Sometimes it's easy to match your identity with those who are around you. In high school I listened to certain types of music because they were popular and dressed a certain way to match everyone else. I watched the same shows as other people and identified with a generation. But it was only after I left school (and most of those relationships) that I discovered a bit of who I really was. I didn't like scary movies after all, and I loved read-

> ## Who Am I?
>
> What type of mom do you want to be? Have you decided? According to Dictionary.com:
>
> identity [ahy-den-ti-tee] the condition of being oneself or itself, and not another: He doubted his own identity.

ing. I learned more about myself in my role as a mom too. Because the truth is, it's nearly impossible to try to look cool or act a certain way when you have been up with a crying baby all night.

If anything, motherhood helps us find who we are because so much that we used to relate to is stripped away. It's a time to make plans—to figure out who you are and where you're going—because it's not just you anymore.

If you don't figure out your life for yourself, you will follow what you know and you'll end up just like your mom or your dad or your friends, because that's what you'll see. Instead, consider motherhood as a chance to appreciate others, but then figure yourself out too. What did your mom do that you liked? What do you want to do differently? Today is the day you can figure it out. Today is the day you can start forming your own identity.

Strengths and Weaknesses

I'm thankful that I had a good mom in so many ways. She was very involved in my life. She volunteered at school dances and took me to tap classes. She believed in me. She always told me I was the best (even though I wasn't). This balanced out my stepdad, who saw me as a bother and who found it easier to ignore me than spend time with me. He also started swinging his fists when he got angry. I'd be fighting with my brother in the back seat, and he'd swing his arm around and *whap!* It was always better sitting behind my stepdad because he couldn't reach around that far.

> The most important thing she'd learned over the years was that there was no way to be a perfect mother and a million ways to be a good one.
>
> — *Jill Churchill,* mystery novelist

Can you guess my strengths and weakness? I'm super involved with my kids, but anger tends to be my biggest issue. I can take a lot and put up with a lot, and then I snap. When I was a young mom I'd find myself slapping my child's shoulder out of frustration. It wasn't as if I was beating him, but I'd smack him harder than I should have. "No! Stop it!" Sometimes I'd flick his cheek or grab his arm too hard.

I remember once I was sitting next to my son and I reached up to brush his hair out of his face and he flinched, as if he thought I was going to hit him. It absolutely broke my heart. I vowed to do things differently. I changed. I stopped that reaction one choice at a time.

It's not that I do things perfectly, but I'm better. Much better. My kids don't know me as a mom who lashes out. But I had to start from the beginning again—praying to God, asking for help and strength, walking away, choosing *not* to react in anger one frustrated moment at a time.

I've learned over the years that I can choose the type of mom I want to be. I choose to be a mom who sits and reads books, who plays games, who makes dinner (even a simple dinner), who sits at the table with her children. I worked to make this my identity.

I choose to take my children to church, and to wait until after they go to bed to watch grown-up shows about grown-up topics. I choose to listen only to music that has positive lyrics. I want to make sure that what my kids are listening to are words that can be repeated.

If you don't make choices about the type of mom you want to be, the choices will pick you, and you'll find yourself amazingly like the people who raised you or the friends you hang out with—for good or bad.

Who Am I?

Like most young moms, when you discovered you were pregnant, many of your roles changed. We're talking dramatic changes. One minute you're walking the mall with friends, and the next you're shopping for diapers and wipes. One day you're comfortable in your skin. The next day your body is swelling and stretching in all the wrong places. You may have attended college and worked two jobs last year, but after having your baby, it's a big accomplishment to get showered and dressed before noon.

With so many adjustments concerning your body, lifestyle, and roles, you may feel as if you haven't processed the changes. You question the person you've become. You also wonder what part the old you plays in your new life.

Identity 1: My Needs

Motherhood. If it was going to be easy, it never would have started with something called labor.

— Old saying

Kids have needs. Moms meet needs.

Striving to meet needs is what mothering is about, right? Everyone talks about the importance of dads, and they are very important, but instinctively, mothers carry most of the load. Of course, if meeting kids' needs were the only ones you worried about, life might not be bad. But there are others with needs too. Our husband or boyfriend. Our parents. Even our friends.

How do we balance the needs of others with our needs?

This is a challenge. Part of our identity will always involve meeting the needs of others. But to what extent? Are you known for giving and giving, without asking for help in return? Do you always put your plans on the shelf when someone else calls with a need?

We have to realize that it's impossible to give constantly. Like a pitcher of water, to be poured out, we first need to be filled up.

I've struggled with this. For many years I made the needs of others my first priority. I cooked my son a second lunch because he didn't like the first one I'd fixed. Or I agreed to babysit for a friend so she could go out. While it's good to help others, there comes a time when we do so much that we crumble. In helping others, I sometimes hurt myself. I was cranky, tired, overwhelmed. Sure, my friends liked that I was always available, but I yelled at my son and let myself fall apart.

We'll talk more about balance later in this book, but I want to make one point: You have to place a priority on your needs, or no one else will. If you don't value yourself, you can be sure others will take advantage of you, whether you're eighteen or eighty!

It's good to meet the needs of others, but care for yourself too. Another way to discover your identity is finding out what *you* need. For some it may be a coffee date with a friend, but for another mom it might be a bath and a book. Remember, when you meet your needs, you're better able to meet the needs of others, especially the needs of your kids.

My Life

My life has changed dramatically. I no longer think about myself but only for my baby. She always comes first. I can't just get up and go anymore because there are always diapers, extra clothes, bottles, and toys that must go too. I can't even go to the bathroom anymore without her coming in and watching.

— Desiree, *Texas*

Identity 2: My Looks

For many of us, the amount of time and money we spend on our looks changes after having a baby. Instead of spending one hundred dollars on clothes or getting my nails done, there are diapers, formula, and wet wipes to buy. "Whether you want to accept it or not, you play a big part in the way other people respond to and treat you," says Jay McGraw, author of *Life Strategies for Teens*. "It all has to do with your behavior, particularly the way you present yourself to the world through your appearance, attitude, actions, and the way you treat others."[1]

What we choose to wear and how we present ourselves makes me think of my third-grade Barbie Halloween costume. My mom bought one of those boxed costumes that had a plastic face with holes for eyes and a mouth-slit to breathe through. It also came with a shimmering pink "gown" that tied in back. I thought I was beautiful … until my face started to sweat under the plastic. It was hard to see, not to mention breathe. I felt like I was suffocating.

After that Halloween, I never wore another plastic-mask costume. However, that didn't stop me from trying to be something I wasn't. It's easy to slip on a "mask." To hide behind a smiling facade. But attempting to be something I'm not doesn't feel good. Doesn't look right. And it's hard to breathe.

I'd like to say that as I grew older, I stopped hiding behind masks. But that wasn't the case. As a high school cheerleader, I always felt like the odd one out. Most of the other girls were a size 0, and I was not. Needless to say, I was always the one on the bottom of the human pyramid! I tried to make up for not being super-thin by wearing all the right clothes and dating a handsome guy. I strove to be popular, and I went to parties even though I really didn't enjoy the atmosphere.

Years later, the masks I wore were updated, but they were still there. After I had my kids, I attempted to be the perfect mom. For instance, I signed my son up for T-ball even though he didn't enjoy it. My three-year-old daughter took ballet, despite the fact that the class was a forty-five-minute drive each way and she couldn't have cared less about dancing. (She did like the tutu, though.)

When I took time to think about my identity, I started asking myself questions. What do I feel comfortable wearing? Where should I focus my time and attention? How would I like to be identified as a person?

I also reconsidered my motives. Why did I go to parties or watch movies that I didn't really care for? Why was I trying to be something I wasn't?

Perhaps you can ask yourself the same questions. Taking time to evaluate your identity will help you fit your life around who you are inside. Not the other way around. When you treat yourself as a valuable person, others will catch on. You're the one in control. It's up to you to decide how you want to be seen and known—without pretending to be something you're not.

My Life

At first, I felt like I had disappointed everyone, and nothing would ever be the same. I thought everyone would look at me like a slut or something. I've learned that what other people think of me isn't as important as what I think of myself. I'll go somewhere now, and people will ask me about the baby—like they're excited and happy for me. I would have never expected that! It really makes me feel good.

— Katherine, *Texas*

Identity 3: What I Am Not

Sometimes the easiest way to discover who we are is to know who we are not.

We are not our children. We all know mothers who go overboard trying to make themselves look good by making their children look great. Just as we don't get report cards for mothering, we also don't get graded on our children's looks or accomplishments. While we want our children to do their best and succeed in life, our self-esteem shouldn't be wrapped up in them.

We are not our mothers. I remember the first time I heard my mother's voice coming out of my mouth. The words "because I told you so" escaped before I had a chance to squelch them.

It's not until we have kids that we truly understand our mothers—all their fretting, their nagging, and their worries. It's also then that we truly understand their love.

Since you are now a mother, it's good to think back on how you were raised. If there were traditions or habits that now seem wise and useful, try them in your parenting. You also have permission to sift out things you now know weren't good. Just because you're a product of your mother doesn't mean you have to turn out just like her. Repeat after me: "I am not my mother."

We are not like any other mother out there. Sometimes you may feel like the world's worst mother. After all, your friend never yells at her son—and sometimes you yell at yours. Then again, your friend may feel bad because you have a wonderful bedtime routine that includes stories and songs. In many cases, the moms you feel inferior to only look like they have it together. All moms feel they don't measure up. Instead of feeling unworthy, we should realize that everyone has strengths and weaknesses. The key is where we place our focus.

The Bible says, "Let's just go ahead and be what we were made to be, without … comparing ourselves with each other, or trying to be something we aren't" (Rom. 12:5–6 MSG).

The problem with comparison is that we always measure our weaknesses against the strengths of others. Instead, we need to thank God for our strengths. We can also ask God to help us overcome our weaknesses—not because we want to compare ourselves or look good in someone else's eyes, but because we want to be the best moms we can be. God knows who he designed us to be, and we need to strive for that.

My Life

My individuality will never end. There will be no one exactly like me, not even my child. She will be like me in some ways, but not at all in others. I wouldn't have it any other way.

— Desiree, *Texas*

Identity 4: I'm Not Who I Was

How different are you today from who you were before you got pregnant? Some moms still have a handle on their old selves. Others feel an ocean of difference separates the two. While it's okay to look back, here are two warnings:

1. Don't dwell on your past identity, believing your greatest achievements are behind you. Instead, realize that having a child doesn't mean you have to kiss your dreams goodbye.

   I learned this as I followed the path to becoming a writer. It was after the birth of my son that I first considered writing for a living. The more I thought about it, the more I realized it made perfect sense. As a child, I loved to read. In middle school, my family lived by a library, and I spent all my free time there.

   When it came to my identity, I could have moped over my past. I could have fretted over my choices. I could have clung to the pain of being abandoned by my old boyfriend. But instead, I decided to look forward, not back. When my son napped or watched cartoons on Saturday mornings, I read books about writing and plunked away on the computer. I put my overactive imagination to good use, creating stories and magazine articles. It was then that I knew my greatest achievements were not in my rearview mirror. It would take hard work, but I had plans for a great future.

2. Don't base your identity on past mistakes. All of us at times wish we could rewind to change our mistakes. We can't, of course. Instead, we can face our regrets in the following ways:

   a. Seek to renew relationships with those you've hurt. If you have an old friend you'd enjoy seeing again, call her up. If you've "had words" with your mom or dad, try to make up. If you've cut other family members out of your life, spend time getting to know them again when appropriate.

   b. Work to overcome bad habits that get you into trouble. You may hate the fact that you used to drink too much, or that you treated people with disrespect. Don't dwell on those regrets. Instead, work to make amends with those you've hurt in the past. Apologize to others for a wrong attitude or bad choices. Even more important, strive to make good choices. Confessing your mistakes to others is a first step, and living differently will prove you've changed and will guide you to success.

c. Consider your past failures as learning experiences for the future. Regrets help us change and make us want to do better. Sure, you've messed up at one time or another. Everyone has. At least you know what not to do!

Identity 5: I Am Unique

Personality is something we're born with. It's something God put in us from the get-go. It's also something that develops as we interact with those around us.

Your personality isn't the only thing that makes you unique. Your looks do too. Maybe you have your mother's eyes or your dad's nose. Your hair might be thick or thin. You may be big boned or tiny. And if you've ever watched those forensic science television shows, you know that you're you down to the smallest part. Baby, you're an original.

And you've been original from day one—as I'm sure your mother has told you. Even as a baby, you had a unique personality and look.

Of course, all of our unique traits are not just random characteristics, thrown together for unknown reasons. To quote Mother Teresa, "How wonderful it is to think that we have all been created for a purpose! We have not come into the world to be a number; we have been created for a purpose, for great things: To love and be loved."

As someone who's worked with teen moms every week, I have something to say to you: You're unique. You may open up to others easily, or it may take a while for you to build a friendship, but you're worth getting to know. You may have a hard time expressing yourself, or maybe it's easy for you to talk. Either way, your words are important. You may be outgoing and cheerful, or you may be quiet and thoughtful. But you have something to offer, just like the young women in our weekly support group have something to offer.

Each teen mom is different, but I think all of you are special. But as much as I love teen moms, there's someone who loves them even more.

In the book *What Every Mom Needs*, authors Elisa Morgan and Carol Kuykendall state, "Our true identity comes not from looking into horizontal mirrors—at reflections of ourselves or our mothers or our past—but looking up at God. As we gaze into his face, we begin to get a true picture of ourselves. He created us in his image."[2]

And just what does God think of you? Yes, you. If he wrote down his opinion of you (which he has), it might come out like this:

- I created her in her mother's womb (Ps. 139:13).
- I delight in her (Zeph. 3:17).
- She has stolen my heart (Song of Songs 4:9).
- I love her (John 3:16).

Now is that cool, or what?

Identity 6: I'm Not Perfect

Use what talents you possess; the woods would be very silent if no birds sang except those that sang best.

— Henry van Dyke, *author*

Many of us wish to grasp perfection. We reach for it, strive for it. And we all fall flat on our faces. Someone once said, "No one is perfect. That's why pencils have erasers." I don't know about you, but I've worn away a few erasers in my lifetime.

Being perfect isn't possible here on earth. There may be people who expect you to be perfect. (Yeah, Mom.) But you've messed up enough to know there's no chance of that. God knows that too. In fact, the whole purpose of God's coming to earth—in Jesus—was to forgive all those troublesome imperfections. When we embrace this gift of forgiveness, our lives are changed. Our future is changed.

"This life was not intended to be the place of our perfection," says author Richard Baxter, "but the preparation for it." When we accept the gift of Jesus' sacrifice, we can look forward to a future with God—on earth and in heaven.

I remember being pregnant at seventeen. I remember trying to figure out what was happening with my body. I remember the crazy emotions. They were up/down, up/down. There were a few emotions that fought to rule above the rest.

Shame and regret battled for first place. Teen pregnancy isn't something you can hide. I had friends who drank. Others did drugs. Some of my friends cheated and lied, but those things were easy to hide. Not so with pregnancy. You can't hide a growing stomach or the baby in, oh, about nine months. Shame was everyone knowing what this "good girl" had been up to. Shame was getting the looks and comments and stares.

Regret was right there too. Regret that I hadn't waited until I was married to have sex. Regret that I didn't have a boyfriend or husband to share in my joy. Regret that I didn't even have my own place. I had just graduated from high school when my son was born. What did I have to offer him?

There were other emotions too, like excitement and anticipation over having a child. I felt bad for having those feelings. I was supposed to be repentant, right? I was supposed to understand the severity of my mistake. I felt guilty for being excited about my baby's birth. Have you ever felt that way?

Having a baby is an exciting thing! You're going to be a mom, and nothing will ever change that. It's exciting to find out who that little person is going to be. A boy? A girl? Will the baby look like you?

Just because you may have made mistakes in your life that led to having a baby at an early age doesn't mean your baby is any less special. If you have a Bible, read Psalm 139 (or look it up at *www.biblegateway.com*). It's my favorite chapter in the Bible.

According to this psalm, God was there when your child was "knit" (made) in a secret place. God knows every moment of your child's life before he or she takes a first breath. God's thoughts for your child are more numerous than the sand on the seashore.

From this moment you may make different choices about many things—about being sexually active or about trying to seek your own pleasure instead of God's plan for your life. It's good to make positive changes. It's also okay to let yourself get excited about this baby … and about being a mom. A new child—God's special creation—is something to celebrate!

Identity 7: I Am Loved

How many movies, books, and songs deal with the topic of love? Countless. In fact, there isn't a topic that's written about or sung about more often. Love is big business.

From the time I was in junior high, I was on the hunt for the perfect guy. I had a few crushes, but they didn't give me the time of day. Then one noticed me. He was more handsome, more wonderful, than I imagined—for the first two months. Then the perfect picture quickly got smudged around the edges.

What to do? I looked for someone else. Someone who would make me feel loved. I don't know why I expected total commitment from someone who wasn't old enough to shave, but I did!

It was an endless cycle. Meet someone, get together, break up. Once I got a little older, the relationships lasted longer—mainly because the physical element was added into the equation. But I soon found out that getting involved physically didn't help the chemistry. It just caused it to be more combustible!

At the time, I would have done anything for that true, everlasting, never-leave-you kind of love. I finally found it years later, but not in a boyfriend. I found it in Jesus, the one who loved me even when I didn't realize it.

In the Bible, John 3:16 says, "For God so loved the world that he gave his one and only Son, that whoever believes in him shall not perish but have eternal life."

Who Am I?

While there are many religions that enforce steps to follow to become holy, there is only one religion that talks about a love you don't earn. When you accept Jesus as Lord, you don't sign up for a list of works. No preaching door to door. No shaving your head and wearing long robes. All you have to do is to believe in Jesus. Jesus who loves you just as you are.

When I fell in love with Jesus, I discovered my true identity. I found out that I'm special. I don't need to dress a certain way or try to be something I'm not. I could be myself, leave behind my regrets, and plan a good future. I didn't need to wear a Barbie mask. I was beautiful just as I was.

And you are too. Have you thought about what a relationship with Jesus would mean for you? Jesus loves you completely, and he sees you as you truly are. He doesn't want you to seek him—to accept him—because there is a list of rules to follow. He wants to spend a lifetime with you, and an eternity beyond that. He wants to show you what the love you've been seeking is all about, through him. He wants to show you your true identity ... and help you be more you than you've ever been.

Who Are You?

Who are you really? Try to describe it in fifty words. Here is my description: "The real me is a mom who enjoys encouraging others, using the talents I was born with, and spending time with those I love and those who love me. I may seem like I have it all together, but the real me prays to God often because I feel weak."

Fifty words exactly! Go ahead, try it.

Some Self-Discovery

Discovering the Unique Me

It's time for self-discovery. Read the following questions, and then write your responses. Don't answer with words that sound good, answers a friend, parent, husband, or boyfriend would like to hear. Answer how you really feel. Hopefully, answering them will help you discover a little more about yourself. Too often we simply rush through life without thinking about our identity and what makes us who we are.

1. If you could choose one person (living or dead) to spend twenty-four hours with, who would it be? Why?
2. If you were given $10,000 and had to spend it in twenty-four hours, what would you buy?
3. If you could model your life after one person you know, who would it be? What qualities do you appreciate about this person?
4. If someone were to describe you, what qualities would you hope they mentioned?
5. If you could log all your thoughts for one day, what would you discover that you think about the most? Are these thoughts mainly positive or negative?
6. If you had a free babysitter for a whole day, what would you do? (Assume your house is clean, you're showered, and you don't need a nap!)
7. Alice Walker once wrote, "She wants to live for once. But doesn't know quite what that means. Wonders if she has ever done it. If she ever will." What does "to really live" mean to you?

Sometimes You Have to Fight

To quote the classic television show *The Wonder Years*, "Change is never easy. You fight to hold on. You fight to let go."

1. What things in your life are you fighting to hold on to?
2. What things are you fighting to let go of?

Moms Help Mold

Identity

My mother said to me, "If you become a soldier, you'll be a general; if you become a monk, you'll end up as the Pope." Instead, I became a painter and wound up as Picasso.

— Pablo Picasso, artist

Think about it. How did your mother help mold your identity, both for the positive and for the negative?

Now, how can you, as a mother, help your child mold his or her identity? Write down three positive things you can do:

1. _____

2. _____

3. _____

Your Words Change Everything

Word Identity

Things Every Child Needs to Hear

- I love you.
- I'm so glad you came into my life. You have made it better.
- There is no one just like you. You are special.
- I adore your smile.
- You fill up a special place in my heart.
- My arms are always open to you.
- You are smart.
- You're extremely huggable.
- I'll always protect you.
- Don't be afraid. I am here.
- You are my greatest treasure.

- If all the children in the world lined up, I would still choose you.
- Well done!

Things Every Young Mom Needs to Tell Herself

- I am a lovely person.
- I am unique and special.
- I'm doing my best to be a good mom.
- It's okay for me to dream.
- All moms need a break.
- I don't need to feel guilty when I take time for myself.
- My good example will make all the difference in the world and to my child.
- I become wise when I seek counsel from wise people.
- It's good to hope for a better future for my child and myself.
- Truth is always the best choice.
- Life looks brighter when I focus on what's really important.
- My habits will become my child's habits, so I'd better choose good ones.
- What I have in the end will never mean as much as who I am.
- There is no greater feeling than when my heart is at peace.
- I don't need to worry about the future. I just need strength for this moment.
- Well done!

Live and Learn

Knowing my identity means knowing my value as a person and a mom.

3

Where Am I Going?

Growth

The hardest thing about being a mom at a young age is how quickly you have to grow up. From the moment I discovered I was pregnant, I had to make a lot of big decisions. I was expected to know what to do with my life, but the truth was I struggled just to make it through each day. I wanted to grow up, I really did, but all my problems trailed along behind me. Not only that, but more problems multiplied by the day. I was expected to support a child and to provide for his physical and emotional needs, yet I still longed for the same type of support. Growth? How? What did that even look like?

What's a young mom to do when she walks into parenting with all the baggage of childhood trailing behind her? Sometimes the best way to grow up is to realize the areas where you need help and to find the right people to help you, like my friend Kayleigh.

Kayleigh was only fifteen years old when she had MaCayla, but she felt as if she'd left her childhood behind long before that.

Looking back on her life, Kayleigh never knew what innocence was. When she was only seven years old, her mom married her stepdad, and his sexual abuse started. He'd try to tell her she was special, but she didn't feel special. The abuse made her feel dirty. The physical abuse that was also present in her home made her feel worse than a dog.

As a child, Kayleigh couldn't depend on anything or anyone. She couldn't guarantee there was food in the cupboard. She couldn't guarantee she'd have decent clothes to wear or that she'd be warm. She couldn't guarantee one day passing without abuse. That rarely happened. And outside of the home things were no better. She couldn't count on friends. She was often teased. The other girls said horrible things about her, and deep down she felt those things were true.

As she grew older, other men approached for sexual favors. Not once in her life had she ever had the power to say no. She didn't know she could.

At just fifteen years old she got a new boyfriend. He was facing his own issues of abandonment, and they seemed to understand each other. Kayleigh felt that if she had a baby, she could leave her mother's home and start her own family. She soon found herself pregnant. But life didn't get easier. She still had to depend on her mom and grandparents for help. Her daughter almost didn't survive the birth, and Kayleigh struggled in her relationship with her boyfriend. Things hadn't gotten easier at all.

Even after becoming a mom, Kayleigh lived the life she saw modeled. She hung out with the wrong people, and she abused alcohol and other substances. She struggled with many things, like anger and a sharp tongue. She was a mother, but she had a lot of growth that needed to happen in her own life. During quiet moments Kayleigh realized that if she didn't change, her daughter would have a tough childhood just like she did, but she didn't know how to change. And her emotions often got the best of her when she tried.

It's easy for others to say, "Grow up," but people often don't understand the struggles you face as a young mom. Just because you have a child doesn't mean all the pain in your past mysteriously vanishes. It doesn't mean you know how to make better decisions overnight.

Growth happens at various levels—physical, emotional, and spiritual—but often the people who look down on teen mothers don't understand the layers of pain and shame that are already there, even at a young age. Many young moms, like Kayleigh, need someone to listen to and support them. They need to be with others who are also in the process of trying to grow as young women and as moms.

Right after her daughter's birth, Kayleigh started attending a Teen MOPS (Mothers of Preschoolers) group. This weekly support group was led by older women who really seemed to care. They told Kayleigh she was important and that she was a child of God with a special purpose. They encouraged her to grow.

More than that, the leaders of the weekly support group displayed character traits like kindness, gentleness, peace, and joy — traits that Kayleigh had never seen up close before. They showed her respect. They taught her the importance of respecting herself. They also brought in speakers who helped the young moms work on specific things that needed to be changed for them to grow. Growth for Kayleigh started when she recognized the areas she needed to change, and then started making changes, no matter how hard they were.

Kayleigh discovered that as she grew in character and skills, she became a good model for her daughter. It wasn't easy. Her anger flared even when she didn't want it to. Sometimes she'd make some positive changes and then revert back to her old ways. The process was long, but as she worked at growth — and sought God's help — she witnessed the changes within. Soon her growth became evident to others too.

Kayleigh was becoming a different person, a person who could provide her children with a safe, healthy home — a home very different from the one where she was raised. Growth changed her, and it soon changed her boyfriend, too, as he sought the same things. They both opened their hearts to God and his work in their lives, and over time the home and family that Kayleigh always dreamed of were hers.

Through this process, Kayleigh learned that God can take the hard stuff, the bad stuff, and turn it around for good. Kayleigh dared to believe that God could heal the hurting places in her heart, and he proved it to be true. The first step in knowing where we're going is recognizing all the places where we need to grow, just like Kayleigh did.

Growth of Character Changes Everything

Show respect even to people who don't deserve it; not as a reflection of their character, but as a reflection of yours.

— Dave Willis, *author and speaker*

Have you ever been around a really beautiful woman—I mean a person whose hair is perfect, whose clothes are stylish, and whose makeup is as flawless as a model's? But then the woman opens her mouth and everything changes. Her ugly words, foul language, anger, pride, or self-centeredness shows up. She's not so pretty anymore, is she? Those looks that drew everyone's attention soon start to pale.

No matter how much time you spend on your appearance, your character is what shines the most. Some of the most caring people I know would not make it into the pages of a glamour magazine, but they are kind and beautiful on the inside.

What type of mom do you want to be? What type of person do you want to be? Do you want to be the most beautiful person inside, or outside?

How you live your life, the words you speak, and the actions you take let everyone know what's really inside. Yet it's hard to hold in the anger and the frustration at times, isn't it? After all, people can be so frustrating and hurtful!

As a teen mom I was hurt over and over again, and I found myself lashing out with unkind words, attitudes, and actions, just like Kayleigh. But I soon realized that the way I was acting wasn't changing anything. People did not start acting better after I cursed them. My anger did nothing to change their opinions. The only one I was hurting by being angry and mean was myself.

No matter what others have done to you, the choices you make in your life are your choices. People can treat you well or they can treat you horribly, but how you respond and how you act are your responsibilities.

It would have been easy for me as a teen mom to get stuck, to point a finger, and to focus on the pain my baby daddy caused when he broke up with me and abandoned our son and me. I wanted a happy family, but things didn't turn out that way. Yet my angry words didn't change my baby daddy. Nothing I could do would change him, so I started changing myself. I started to grow.

I could have filled my life with hate, but instead I chose to do things differently with God's help. With a lot of prayer and seeking God's ways, I chose to make myself better. I did it for me. I did it for my child.

My son has never met his biological dad, but God brought an awesome man into his life to be a dad. This good man came into my life because of the changes that happened within me. I sought God and I asked him to change me from the inside out. I was always a pretty young woman, but that was only outward beauty. Once I decided I needed to grow and to change, beauty grew from within, and someone special noticed—a guy who was also beautiful inside and out. John was kind, gentle, and had peace.

Don't get me wrong, John is no wimp. He'd been in a special unit in the Marine Corps. He is tall, masculine, and tough. Yet he is trustworthy and truthful. He is someone I can trust with my heart.

Not every young mom will have a great guy show up right away. Some may spend many years looking for the right guy. But don't give up, and don't lower your standards. Think of the type of person you can trust with your heart. Make a list of the qualities that you won't compromise.

Also, consider what type of person *you* need to be to attract that type of person. Think of your dream guy. What is he looking for? Someone who is kind and generous? Who cares for others and is diligent in her work and parenting? Growth is becoming that person with God's help.

If I would have stayed angry, mad, foul-mouthed, and spiteful, I would not have attracted a caring and considerate man. As I've turned my life over to God, I've become a better person and a better mom, one day at a time. I not only attracted a person who loves me unconditionally, I've also lived a life that has been a good example to my son. My son is kind, happy, and caring, and he learned that from what he saw in our home.

God brought me a caring person to spend my life with. God has taken care of my son too. God will *always* be there for you when you turn to him. It starts by taking all that pain and anger and turning it over to God. Yes, you've been hurt, but you don't have to deal with it by yourself. In fact, God wants to deal with it for you.

When we forgive people, it doesn't mean that we allow them to continue to hurt us. If you're in a situation where you're being hurt emotionally or physically, you need to leave it. Leave the situation, and you also leave the bitterness behind. How?

Forgiveness doesn't mean that the pain will never bother you again. Instead, it means to give the wrong done against you to God and let him deal with it. That means that God will handle the situation for you. He will give the person his or her just reward.

I don't know about you, but it's scary to me to think that God is going to "handle me." To forgive someone is to tell God, "This person hurt me, but I'm going to let you handle it." And then you have to let it go. The memories won't go away, but every time they come up you can tell yourself, "I still feel the pain. I still feel the hurt, but I'm giving it to God (again) to handle." It's turning it all over to him again, and again, and again.

I know it's hard to act pretty when you've been hurt. You want to lash out at others and hurt others, just as they've hurt you. And that's the key. Forgiveness is not about acting pretty. That acting job will take you only so far. It has to go deeper. It has to go all the way to your heart.

I choose to put God's Word into my mind and heart so that peace and joy flow out. What goes in is what comes out of your life. God's Word, truth, love, hope, peace, and kind thoughts are things that make me beautiful when I tuck them deep inside.

Also, when you let your emotions run wild and you let the ugliness out, your kids are watching. Even when they're babies, they're watching everything you do. They learn to talk the way you talk. They learn to walk, and eat, and talk on the phone, and use the toilet because they're watching you. And they learn to act and react too.

Living a good life and being a good mom, having joy and peace, is the way I've *won*. I win by not letting someone else pull me down to his or her level. I win by controlling myself and my attitude. I also win by moving beyond the level of those who've hurt me, and I've become a better person despite all the wrong done to me. I've become a better mom.

Now, what about you? What are you putting in your mind and heart? Good thoughts? Forgiveness? God's Word? Or are you still allowing anger and pain to run rampant? What you put in is what will come out.

What are you expecting to come out?

Being willing to grow in maturity and character is the first step. Only then will you be able to grow in other areas. You can't do great things if your life is filled with anger and unforgiveness. Take care of those things first, and you're off to a great start!

Growth Doesn't Mean Perfection (That's Not Possible)

As a pregnant teen, the pressure not to fail at raising my child was intense. I noticed the people watching me. Because of those stares, I wanted to make sure I did everything right. I wanted to have the perfect kid so people would see that a young mom could succeed.

If I could go back and do things differently, I would relax more. I wanted my son to be the smartest at preschool. In T-ball I wanted him to be the best player. He was pretty smart and could beat me at memory games by age three, but as for sports, well, he was more interested in staring at the clouds than catching a ball.

I wanted to be seen as the perfect mom too. I kept my house spotless. I thought growth meant that I should be perfect.

I started writing and publishing, and I tried to become a success. By this time I lived 2,000 miles from those who knew me as a teen mom, but that didn't stop me from striving. I didn't go on enough nature walks or play catch very often because I was too busy keeping my world in order.

What I know now is that my world will never be perfect. My to-do list will never be done. My son is now grown, married, and has a baby and a toddler of his own. He's not perfect, I'm not perfect, and perhaps some of our favorite memories are from times when we forgot there was a world out there we were trying to impress and just enjoyed being together—laughing, loving, and enjoying life.

Maybe you're like me. Maybe you feel everyone's eyes on you, watching to see if you will succeed or fail. First of all, the most important thing is not to worry about those opinions. Still, that doesn't mean you don't try. Do try. Do take growth steps, but don't feel as if you have to be perfect. No one ever can. Know that starting small is okay. Whatever you do, don't put your dreams and goals up on a shelf.

My Life

I tried to compensate by volunteering and being on as many committees as I could (it was Head Start). I still never "fit in." I felt like the other moms still regarded me as a "kid." I didn't make any friends but I did get some awesome experience to pad my resume with.

— Mari, *Montana*

Overwhelmed by the responsibility of having to make all the decisions, having to provide for my son and plan for the future with no instruction manual to refer to. I feel frustrated because I have such high ideals as to what kind of mother I want to be, but I can't seem to live up to them.

— Simone, *New Zealand*

I am certainly not saying raising children is a piece of cake, because it isn't. But support is so important. Insight and advice from others, whether your parents, friends, neighbors, etc. They help so much to keep us from being stuck on one idea.

— Marjie, *Montana*

Life Lived on Hold (Sort Of)

We all learn by experience, but some of us have to go to summer school.

— Peter DeVries, *author*

Have you ever heard the sentiment, "When you hold that little baby in your arms, the whole world stands still"? In a way, that phrase is true. With a child, there is no saying, "You can wait." There is no silencing the constant demands. There's no putting him away on a shelf, to bring down at a more convenient time.

Instead we use the shelf in other ways. That's where we stash our dreams, our plans, and our desires. It's the highest shelf. Out of reach.

Some young moms question if their dreams still make sense. When stacked up next to reality, dreams often seem foolish. Should I even try to grow and to follow my dreams? Who cares about your desire to become a journalist when you have to put food on the table?

After becoming a mom, sometimes simple goals are all we can handle—making it to work on time or having the groceries last until payday. With feedings, naps, and diapers, who has time to dream?

My Life

I'm a stay-at-home mother at the moment, and I'm hoping to get a job in the next few months. It's overwhelming because no one wants to hire a teen mum, or young mum, around here. Some people even look at me weird, but I guess that's how it goes.

— Sarah, Australia

At the time I found out I was pregnant, I was collecting information to attend school in Washington, D.C., specifically looking into the CIA. (I had been invited the year prior and spent a week on a tour checking into various job opportunities to finalize my decision.) Just thinking back on this makes me wonder.

— Marjie, Montana

Still, as noted earlier, a young mom longs to know her efforts are significant. She needs to feel that her mothering and her life matter. She also requires a sense of identity—knowing who she is and who she's meant to be.

So even though it's hard to make changes, remember that they're important. Also remember that they don't happen all at once. They happen one small step at a time, in baby steps. Ready?

Baby Steps

When you want to spruce up your body, you can exercise, get a new haircut, or put on makeup. Yet there's no foundation or mascara to make the inside shine. (Oh, how I wish there were!)

"I am always doing that which I can not do, in order that I may learn how to do it," said the artist Pablo Picasso. In the same way that Picasso learned his art bit by bit, our taking baby steps toward patience, gentleness, and consideration helps us grow into those character traits over time.

In my early parenting years, there were days when I couldn't tell if I was making any progress in my character growth. Especially the days when the money ran out, the baby was sick, or the neighbor was grumpy. Then I displayed character traits I did not want my child to copy.

Inside I wanted to follow the teachings of the Bible. I attempted to treat others as I wished to be treated. I longed to be thankful for all God had given me. Yet my growth reminded me of the game Mother May I. I took three baby steps forward and two giant leaps back.

It was helpful to continually look to positive role models and caring mentors for encouragement and inspiration. If they could do it, with God's help, I could too.

As I read the Bible I also learned that I have another mentor who is always able to provide guidance: Jesus Christ. I can read about his loving interaction with others in the Bible. A good place to start is in Matthew, Mark, Luke, and John, books named after the men who wrote them. You can't get a more perfect role model than Jesus. And as you follow him, you will grow in many ways!

Growth Benefits Your Family

I once had a plaque hanging in my kitchen that said, "When Mama ain't happy, ain't nobody happy." How true! Your attitude plays a big part in the attitude of your home. Those around you, especially your children, will pick up hints on how to act and react in this world.

If you've been a mother for any time at all, you've probably figured out that almost everything you do will be copied. A building block held to your child's ear becomes a phone. A toy car pointed toward the TV becomes a remote control. Your frequent expressions, such as *No!* or *Stop that*, will be repeated.

Also, consider the way you respond to things. When your child knocks over a glass of milk, you can either yell or you can clean it up and tell her everyone makes mistakes. The situation doesn't change, but the outcome makes a big difference.

Our attitudes as moms improve when we have time for inward growth. When a mom has a chance to read a book or sketch a picture during a lazy afternoon, building on her talents, she'll feel better and her family will benefit.

This means, as hard as it is, moms need time to dream, plan, and grow. While it may seem impossible (especially since you're balancing work, school, friends, family, and mothering), take a few minutes each day to think about (1) who you want to be, and (2) how you can get there. Allow your mind to wander as you take a shower or drift off to sleep. This "think time" will encourage inner growth that will benefit all areas of your life, especially your attitude toward your family.

My Life

I haven't played my beloved guitar in over a year. And art? What art? As for other outlets, I'm pouring my juices into starting a club at school for other parent-students. I think it's a worthwhile cause, and I'm fighting for it.

— Amanda, *Ontario, Canada*

Growth Benefits Your World

Anne Frank, known for her World War II diary, once wrote, "How wonderful it is that nobody need wait a single moment before starting to improve the world." It's important to impact your family and community, but sometimes God will use you to change your world too.

Growing up, my friend Nicole always believed she'd spend her life helping other people. Then, as a young teen, she was date raped and it totally derailed her. She went to Teen Challenge to help her deal with some of her problems, and Nicole returned home, graduated from high school at age fifteen, and then started Bible college. A few years later Nicole got derailed again, and she ended up pregnant. She was kicked out of Bible college and thought she could never be used to help other people. But God had other plans.

Once she turned her life back over to him, God allowed Nicole to help others, just as she always wanted. She's a youth leader, speaker, radio host, and writer. She has a ministry called *Choose Now* that helps teens and parents (*http://nicoleodell.com/*).

When you grow, you not only benefit yourself, but you also can impact your world, just like Nicole. And you don't have to start big. Here are simple ways to start:

1. Thank a friend who has helped you.
2. Make and take a card to someone who needs encouragement.
3. Get together with another young mom for encouragement and support.
4. Spend ten minutes reading to your baby.
5. Offer to watch a friend's baby so she can pursue a dream.
6. Help a friend with her homework.
7. Bake a cake for someone you care about—just because.
8. Hug someone who's encouraged you.
9. Introduce yourself to another young mom at the park or at McDonald's.
10. Bring other young moms together for encouragement and support.

Which one will you try first? Circle it!

Your Growth Is a Gift to God

"Thank you for making me so wonderfully complex! Your workmanship is marvelous … You watched me as I was being formed … You saw me before I was born…. Every moment was laid out before a single day had passed" (Ps. 139:14–16 NLT).

This passage blows me away. Not only does God love me, he thinks I'm a work of art. He likes the way he made me. He had a plan for my life before I was even born. When I allow myself to grow, I transform into the person he designed me to be.

Dannah Gresh, author of *Secret Keeper*, puts it this way: "You were created as a masterpiece and you are one of God's expressions of beauty. Short, tall, thin, thick, freckles, big eyes, small ones … it doesn't matter."[1]

Thinking about God's purpose for me—for my growth—reminds me of the house plans I once drew in my high school drafting class. I sketched a design for an amazing three-story house with large pillars out front. The kitchen sparkled with enough elegance to host a Food Network cooking show. The dining room sprawled big enough to hold the studio audience. But my favorite part of the blueprint was the tub in the master bathroom. I drew that thing big enough to sink up to my neck.

Instead of sketching a dream house, imagine your dream life.

- Who do you enjoy spending time with?
- What do you appreciate most?
- What makes you feel at ease, at rest?
- What sparks your creativity?
- What lights a fire under you and makes you want to accomplish big things?

Find a journal and write these things down. Also write down ways you can grow in each of these areas. Go back to your list often and allow yourself to dream. It'll encourage your growth!

God Wants to Grow Us Too

Maybe you've had a hard time answering these questions. Or maybe the answers seem about as exciting as a half-deflated balloon. Do you want more meaning to your life than just being comfortable? If so, I have good news! For thousands of years, smart people from around the world have been asking about the meaning of life—their personal lives too.

The Bible has had the answer all along. "It's in Christ that we find out who we are and what we're living for. Long before we first heard of Christ and got our hopes up, he had his eye on us, had designs on us for glorious living, part of the overall purpose he is working out in everything and everyone" (Eph. 1:11 MSG).

Or to put it another way, "The easiest way to discover the purpose of an invention is to ask the creator of it," says Rick Warren, author of *The Purpose-Driven Life*. "The same is true for discovering your life's purpose: Ask God."

Don't tuck away the blueprint of your life in a dusty drawer. Living up to your potential is a gift—to yourself, to your family, and to the one who created you.

What were you created for? Ask the one who knows.

Growing Pains

I remember the first time my son realized he had grown taller. He was two and was knocked off his feet—literally. One month he'd been able to run under the dining room table with ease. The next month his head connected with the hard wood, which sent him sprawling.

Perhaps you remember a similar growth spurt in your life when your arms and legs stretched faster than you had learned to use them. I remember as a child waking up as my muscles and bones ached and attempting to stretch farther than was comfortable.

Then there were times when I was growing in all the wrong places, such as during pregnancy. T-shirts failed to cover my expanding abdomen, allowing my belly button to peek out. My jeans no longer fit. My life didn't fit either.

Growing into a responsible parent can be painful too. College classes stretch us. Finding new friends makes us feel uncomfortable and awkward. And like a young child who needs to learn to duck his head, you have to understand that you're different than before. Growth means stretching your hours, your focus, and your abilities.

You may feel like you can't make it to the end of the day. Growth is learning to push through it. Do it anyway. Prove yourself.

Before you became a mom, finishing a term paper on time might not have been a big deal. Now it's a reason to be proud of yourself. Growth means meeting challenges you never thought you could face, like graduating from high school, getting your driver's license, or finishing the art class you've dreamed about taking.

It also means making a commitment to yourself. (Yes, I can do this.) Growth means stepping out of your comfort zone and into your courage zone.

My Life

After facing the idea that I was pregnant, my next obstacle was to get through my summer classes. I did an archaeological dig for weeks nine to fifteen of my pregnancy. It was rough because it was so hot and humid on the site, but I made it. Everyone was shocked that I had done that. They couldn't imagine working through morning sickness and the exhaustion of the dig. I felt like Superwoman for that.

— Amanda, *Ontario, Canada*

Moving at a Snail's Pace

Have you ever watched a flower grow? First, you see a tiny shoot. Then a bud begins to form. The green nub starts to open, and soon you see bits of color. Before you know it, the flower unfolds. It's perfectly formed, offering beauty and fragrance.

But growth in humans is much more complicated. Growth not only involves the body, it also involves your mind, your emotions, and your spirit.

Physical growth is the easiest to see, especially in your child. Your baby may seem to grow like a weed (which grows twice as fast as a flower). But for yourself, you may question whether you're changing and improving at all. Like a 4x4 monster truck bogged down in the mud, you feel stuck. Worse yet, you're spinning your wheels with no progress.

I have a friend who measures her children's growth on a wall in their hallway. At least a dozen times I've watched her children flatten their backs against the wall to see if they've grown—sometimes more than once in a day! What adults realize, but kids may not, is that growth takes time. A yardstick or lines on the wall can't measure the internal growth we seek.

Remember that when you seek growth, you need to give yourself time. Don't expect changes overnight. Be patient with yourself, and be patient with others. Also, in addition to time, growth is costly. But in the end it'll be worth the cost. I promise.

Costly Choices

Choice means cost. The choice to stay up late will cost you sleep. The choice to attend a night class at your local college costs money and time spent away from friends or family. The choice to take a walk in the park instead of cooking dinner means having peanut butter and jelly again. The same is true when we work on our internal growth—there's always a price tag. The question to ask is, What will it cost to achieve my dreams?

Perhaps you feel the cost of your dreams is too high for this moment in your life. Consider becoming a taster. For example, you might not have the money to attend a fine art academy, but you could sign up for a pottery class at your local community college.

My friend Jessica has always dreamed of becoming a professional photographer, but with small kids at home she felt it was unrealistic to start her own business. Instead of forgetting about her dreams, Jessica uses her kids as models for practice. It's a picture-perfect opportunity! In the future she hopes to open her own studio, but until then Jessica focuses on improving her craft.

What do you dream about doing? What can you do to make your dreams a reality? Take a minute and think about how your choices either move you toward your dream or away from it. They do.

There's a Dream in My Heart

Dreaming can't be done well while you're changing dirty diapers or hurrying off to work. But there may be moments for dreaming that you haven't thought about. When you're up at night rocking your baby, let your mind wander and take a few minutes to dream. Instead of turning on the television or checking out Facebook on your phone, let your mind walk through the next steps that you need to take toward your dream. Or, when you're putting on your makeup, think of your "make up." What makes you who you are? This means putting on a detective's hat and looking for clues in your character.

When you were younger, you may have had a hard time deciding what you wanted to be when you grew up, as most kids do. One day you wanted to be a teacher, the next day a lawyer. You still may question what you want. The key is concentrating on the one passion you find yourself returning to. If you could choose one thing to do with your life, what would it be?

Get out the magnifying glass and consider where you've been and where you're going. Sleuth around your home and your life and consider what things are important to you. Is it caring for others, being artistic, or using your brain to solve problems?

Here are some questions to start:

- What do I enjoy doing?
- What qualities do I appreciate about myself?
- Do I like working with people or working alone?
- When I look back twenty years from now, what accomplishments will I be the most proud of?

Answering these questions will help you figure out what dreams are most important.

Growing through Education

A good education is one thing that many young moms dream about. Education helps us be smart, well-rounded people. As a young parent, your education may have been one of the first things to suffer. Attending classes while raising a child is tough. I know.

I clearly remember staying up, after a long day of parenting, to work on math homework. But I can see now how my education was important. Finishing high school opens up doors to college.

So where are you in your educational process? I know many young moms who have gone on to graduate from high school and college. The key is making a plan. So let's make one:

- Write down your three top educational needs.
- Write down three possible solutions for each need.

Example:

Need: To get my high school diploma or equivalent.
Options: Local high school, community college classes, GED course, homeschool, and other alternative schools.

After you know your needs and think of solutions, the next thing to do is to make a plan of action. Ready to start?

Your Plan of Action

Excellence can be achieved if you risk more than others think is safe, love more than others think is wise, dream more than others think is practical, and expect more than others think is possible.

— Anonymous

To dream is to plan. To dream big is to put that plan in writing and take small steps to achieve your goal. Many coaches and consultants use the acronym SMART to explain goal setting. SMART refers to goals that are Specific, Measurable, Achievable, Realistic, and Time-framed.

Let's take a closer look:

- *Specific*. Pick a large goal. Is it finishing school? Finding a better-paying job? Next, break that into specific smaller goals. Once you have your list, choose one thing you can accomplish this week.
- *Measurable*. Mark off your achievements as you complete them. The check marks on the page prove you're making progress.
- *Achievable*. Don't set yourself up for failure. Pick small goals you can complete in a short period of time. Then use the small goals as stepping stones to the larger ones.
- *Realistic*. Be honest with yourself. How much time will you need to reach this goal? What talents will you have to develop? Are you willing to commit?
- *Time-framed*. Set time limits for your goals. Deadlines give a sense of urgency. You can do it!

Growth Involves Sharing Your Dream

Once you've settled on a plan, the best recipe for success is to find a partner to help keep you on track. Choose someone you trust and respect. Take time to share your goals with this person, but also be sure to listen to her goals. The key to an accountability partner is consistency. Try to talk at least once a week to discuss your progress and to spur each other on.

When I first desired to be a writer, I connected with another young mom named Cindy who had the same dream. Since I was often stuck home without a car, we spent time discussing our dreams over the phone. Because of our mutual encouragement, we've both seen our dreams become reality.

Remember that the best type of accountability partner is a friend. Look for someone who is encouraging and future-minded. Think about this friend as your personal devoted fan. Someone to tell you that you can do it. Someone to be your dream keeper.

Create Yourself

As a final thought, realize that to live as a mother is to live with change. Each day consists of moments of learning and growth. For our children, growth can be measured in inches and pounds, but as a mother, growth means choosing who we want to be and seeking God's help.

In the Bible, Proverbs 16:9 says, "In his heart a man plans his course, but the Lord determines his steps" (NIV 1984).

Your life is like a lump of clay, ready to be formed into something beautiful. The same God who placed your interests and dreams in you can help you see them through.

Dreams and Goals

I was talking with my friend and she mentioned she wanted to become a writer. Her words stirred something inside me, and I knew that's what I wanted to do too. What do you want for your future? What's something that you feel made to do? Here's an exercise to help you figure it out. Write down your answers. Think through your dreams and goals. Pray about them.

Your Name: _____ Today's Date: _____

Three to Six Months
1. What is one way I can improve myself over the next few months?
2. What can I do to be a better mom?

3. What is something I need to commit to pray about?
4. Who would I like to build a better relationship with? How can I start?
5. What can I do in the next few months that will help my future?

Six to Twelve Months

1. How do I imagine myself in a year?
2. What will my life as a mom be like one year from now? How can I make it better?
3. What can I do to prepare for that improved person?
4. What one Scripture verse can I memorize to help me grow?
5. What relationships do I need to walk away from? Who is holding me back from becoming the person I want to be?
6. What can I start today that will help me plan for my career path?

Beyond Twelve Months

1. How can I become a more positive impact in my church over the next year?
2. What does God desire for my future?
3. Who can encourage me on my path?
4. How can I improve my relationship with my parents?
5. What friends will help me grow in my faith? In what ways can I help them grow?

Five Years from Now

1. Where do I see myself? In college? In a career?
2. How do I see my life as a mom in five years?
3. What positive steps can I take to get there?
4. What type of person do I need to be to attract the man of my dreams?
5. How can I pray for that future husband?

These are just a few things to get you started. Feel free to talk about these with your friends or your mentors! The more we think, plan, and pray, the closer we will get to achieving God's dreams — wonderful dreams — for our lives and the lives of our children!

Keep Track to Look Back

Monitor Your Growth

Talk is cheap. Words are plentiful. Deeds are precious.

— H. Ross Perot, *former presidential candidate*

Just like growth marks on the wall, you need to mark where you've been to see how much you've grown. In the process of change and exploration, consider using one or all of the following ideas to monitor your progress:

- *Journaling*. Keep a notebook of your thoughts. Jot down the progress you're making in your growth and the various feelings you experience on your journey.
- *Mementos*. My windowsill near my desk is cluttered with mementos — photos of special days, ticket stubs from events, trinkets I've picked up during various trips. These are special reminders that I'm moving in the right direction.
- *Create a growth chart*. Are you familiar with growth charts for infants? You can create your own growth chart for your goals. Use lined paper to keep track of days and months. Then record your progress. You can record character goals, such as going a week without using a curse word. Or personal goals, such as checking the want ads for a new job. Mark down your progress, and then reward yourself. (Five small goals accomplished can equal one tall latte!)

Time to Grow

A Well-Balanced Life

Growth includes all areas of your being: body, mind, emotions, and spirit. How well are you taking care of yourself? Are you covering all the bases? A well-balanced life may be hard with a new baby or a child. It doesn't matter if you get it all right, but small steps get you headed in the right direction!

- *Body*. Are you taking care of your body? Do you get enough rest? Do you exercise? Do you drink plenty of water? Are you making healthy choices? Are you choosing foods that fuel your body?
- *Mind*. Are you giving your mind what it needs? Do you take time to explore your interests or to learn something new? Have you made time to read a good book? Do you take time to dream, and to share these dreams with a friend?
- *Emotions*. Are you honest with yourself about your emotions? Do you share how you truly feel with someone who cares? Do you let yourself cry? Do you take time for fun?
- *Spirit*. Do you take time to think about God and about what you mean to him? Do you pray? Do you spend time considering how the truths in the Bible affect your life?

Live and Learn

Growing as a person will create a brighter future for my child and myself.

4

Do You Love Me?

Intimacy

The body is a house of many windows: there we all sit, showing our-selves and crying to the passers-by to come and love us.

— Robert Louis Stevenson, *poet*

I didn't know what I was thinking. I wasn't thinking, that is for certain. I saw my baby daddy in town. It was a random meeting. He told me to call him, and I did.

This was the person with whom I'd had an on-again, off-again relationship for three years, but as soon as I told him that I was pregnant, he broke up with me and was with somebody else. But a glimmer of hope flamed inside. Maybe he did love me after all. Maybe I *was* worthy in his eyes.

We talked for just a few minutes. He told me to come over, that he wanted to talk about our son. I knew he was lying. He didn't care about our son at all, but I was drawn to him. It was like two sides of a powerful magnet being pulled together. I started to tell him about Cory, but he only seemed to be half listening. Soon he was kissing me, and it seemed so right—and so very wrong. I was dating someone else by this time. Someone who really loved me. I had also started living for God, and I knew that this old relationship was no good for me. I knew it would lead me to make bad decisions. My heart would be broken again and again.

When I left his house that day, guilt plagued me, and I wondered what was wrong with me. Why would I do that? Why did I let him draw me in? Why couldn't I break free from his hold?

What I didn't realize then was the invisible bond that we had built over time. God made it that way. His plan was for one man and one woman to be married and united for life, so that their times of intimacy and lovemaking would bond them together. The problem comes when we take matters into our own hands and step outside of God's perfect plan. I became sexually active at a young age, bonding myself to another person. I dated a few other guys, and I just assumed that a sexual relationship was something I needed to do. After all, that's what everyone on television did. That's what all the popular musicians sang about too.

I had no idea at the time how I was hurting myself. Sexual bonds aren't meant to be broken, and having them be torn in two after a breakup crushed my heart. I longed for intimacy—for someone to know me and love me completely—but it hurt to pursue it. Soon I found myself putting up a wall around my heart, not letting anyone in, including my son for a time. I loved him, but in a way, it was at a distance. It was almost as if I was afraid to even let him too close.

What is wrong with me? I thought again as I drove away from my baby daddy's home. It took me a few years to figure out the answer. I had been looking for love in all the wrong places, and my heart didn't know what to feel anymore.

There's More to Intimacy Than Sex

One main reason we choose to have sex is our desperate search for intimacy, but true intimacy is usually the last thing we find. Sexually active, we seek a lasting commitment but end up with heartbreak.

Another side effect of the search for intimacy through sex is we have a hard time learning other ways to relate. We miss the joy of heart bonds because society has fed us a lie that physical bonding is the only way to truly connect.

Do You Love Me?

Think about it: in today's movies, how do you know if two people are "in love"? They have sex with each other. While this may be an easy way to show attraction on the big screen, this isn't the real world. True intimacy is made possible by the use of relationship skills and not as a result of sex drives.

I know I had the wrong ideas about intimacy when I was young. I thought that "going all the way" was the only way to show a guy that I truly loved him.

- 2% of teens have had sex by the time they reach their twelfth birthday.
- 16% of teens have sex by age 15.
- 33% of teens have sex by age 16.
- 48% of teens have sex by age 17.
- 61% of teens have sex by age 18.
- 71% of teens have sex by age 19.[1]

Think back:

- What type of messages about attracting guys, getting guys, and having sex did you receive?
- How did these messages affect you?
- Did you feel you weren't complete without a boyfriend?
- What do you wish you would have known about guys and sex when you were younger?

Me too!

I often see young moms making the same mistakes I made. They are looking for love, and sometimes they make decisions and choose boyfriends based on what is easiest at the moment. A young mom may think, *Here's a guy who likes me. He likes my kid too. He may not be exactly what I'm looking for, but he's a whole lot better than nothing.*

Some young moms are willing to compromise because the guy fills their need for companionship. But have you ever heard the saying, "Don't shop when you're hungry"? The same can be said about dating. Don't "shop" when you have an inner hunger that is desperate for a relationship. Otherwise you may end up with pork rinds when what you really need is a nice T-bone steak!

My advice to young moms who are looking for a companion is this: Wait for someone special who is better than just good enough. Out there, somewhere, is a guy who is your best. You are beautiful enough and smart enough to get the attention of many men. But don't waste your time trying different ones on like someone searching for the perfect bathing suit. Instead, look for, dream of, and wait for that special person.

Do you know a friend who throws around the word "forever" without really meaning it? Here is a humorous story that shows how sometimes people don't really mean it when they say forever.

"The owner of a photographic studio tells the story of a college boy who came in with a framed picture of his girlfriend. He wanted the picture duplicated. In removing the photograph from the frame, the studio owner noticed the inscription on the back, written by the girlfriend: 'My dearest Tommy: I love you with all my heart. I love you more and more each day. I will love you forever and ever. I am yours for all eternity.' It was signed 'Dianne' and contained a P.S.: 'If we should ever break up, I want this picture back.'"[2]

Too often when it comes to relationships, we're blind to what's obvious to those around us. A bad pick is easier to see in someone else's relationship than in our own. We easily notice the faults in our friend's boyfriend, but we are blind to the faults in our guy.

After a bad breakup, young moms often find themselves saying, "I should have listened to my mom or my friend. They could see what he was like all along."

"Whenever the truth is threatening, we tend to reach for the blinders," says author Jo-Ellen Dimitrius.[3] It's time to take off those blinders and take a good look. Who are you choosing? Can he be considered your best? If not, why are you settling for less?

If you are currently in a dating relationship, ask yourself how you would view your boyfriend if you were an outsider looking in. Are you sticking around because you're needy? Because of fear? The people with the biggest needs or fears are usually the ones who fill their lives with the biggest Mr. Wrong.

Also, our judgment in relationships disappears when sex is thrown into the mixture. Once the powerful and pleasurable ingredient of sex is added, we tend to overlook even basic flaws—until the passion subsides, of course. But by then it can be too late. By then, your emotions are knotted tight.

Real Life "Love"

The messages in teen magazines for young girls are obvious: Winning a boyfriend is crucial, so you need to dress skimpy, approach guys boldly, and don't think twice about going all the way!

Yet what does that mean in real life? It may mean broken hearts and bad reputations. It may mean unplanned pregnancies or sexually transmitted diseases. One statistic even states that unmarried, teenage girls who are sexually active are three times more likely to be depressed than girls who are not sexually active! Also, girls who are sexually active are almost three times more likely to attempt suicide than are girls who are not sexually active.[4]

Also, most sexually transmitted diseases cannot be cured. The symptoms can be managed, but the disease itself will be with you forever. And you will pass it on when you meet the person you want to spend your life with.

I won't spend a lot of time on this. I'll just say three things:

1. Sexually transmitted diseases can happen anytime you have sex. Human papillomavirus (HPV) is the most common sexually transmitted infection in the United States. HPV is so common that nearly all sexually active men and women get it at some point in their lives.[5] It's much more likely that you'll get a sexually transmitted disease than that you'll get pregnant. And, if you are a teen mom, the odds are *really* high, since you already beat the odds once by having a baby.[6]

2. If any part of your private parts touches any part of your boyfriend's private parts, you are exposed. The only safe sex is *not*

having sex! Condoms do not protect you from sexually transmitted diseases, no matter what anyone tells you. Even more important, condoms do not protect your heart or your emotions.

3. It *can* happen to you. I've met two young moms who had cervical cancer at the age of eighteen due to a sexually transmitted disease. *Cancer*. My heart breaks over what they had to face at such a young age. I know that many young moms didn't think they'd end up pregnant, but they did. Getting a serious sexually transmitted disease or cancer can happen to you too.

Perhaps it's time to take a closer look at the messages the media is telling young women. It's not possible to have sex without consequences, no matter how romantic it appears on television and in movies.

All about Intimacy

The easiest kind of relationship for me is with ten thousand people. The hardest is with one.

—Joan Baez, *folk singer*

What do you think of when you hear the word *intimacy*? Often, it is used as a nice way to say sex. Such as, "We were intimate last night." While this is one definition, intimacy is so much more. Here's how Webster's dictionary defines it: "The state of being intimate; close familiarity or association; nearness in friendship." The dictionary is a good place to start, but let's go deeper into what intimacy is and what it looks like.

Intimacy may mean holding hands with that special guy, knowing you don't need to speak. Or it can be those times when a husband and wife share their bodies in ways they will never share with anyone else.

Sometimes we feel the most intimate when we are at our worst. A friend of mine, Marie, became sick and was hospitalized soon after she started dating a man. Even though they'd known each other only a few weeks, he came to visit her in the hospital every night—just to sit beside her while she slept. He also took care of her cats and even washed her laundry. It wasn't the most romantic way to begin a relationship (for sure!), but the kind way he comforted Marie, helped her, and accepted her at her worst created an intimacy that a dozen candlelight dinners couldn't touch. They eventually married.

Friendships can also be one of the best settings for intimacy. Sometimes you just need someone to talk to about the stuff that guys just don't think about (such as makeup, stretch marks, and labor stories). A good friend will listen to your struggles and successes, and she understands when you don't want to talk, preferring just to hang out.

A loving family can be another source of intimacy. After all, who else can jump on your little brother's bed to wake him up? Who else knows how your mom likes her coffee?

Intimacy does not, should not, happen with only one person. No one person is able to meet all our needs. Our friends provide a type of support that is different from a husband's or a boyfriend's. If we expect another person to provide all the love and friendship we need, we're usually in for a rude awakening.

My Life

I live with my parents-in-law, and my husband won't even sleep in the same bed with me. Intimacy ends up being a morning kiss.

— Amanda, *Ontario, Canada*

Intimacy is something that is shared between two people. Something special like a good book or secret, and not necessarily sex.

— Desiree, *Texas*

Intimacy means having someone who you can confide in and trust. Someone who is always there for you.

— Jessica, *Florida*

Here's another popular definition of intimacy: "Into-me-see." When we are intimate with someone, it's as if we're handing that person spy goggles to look into our souls. It also means looking into the soul of another. Intimacy is a two-way street, so if you want a clear view of another person, you must first offer a glimpse of yourself.

But building an intimate relationship is not something that happens overnight. "Intimacy—genuine intimacy—is not immediate. We expect it to be. The world around us tells us it is," says author Elisa Morgan. "Singles walk into bars and come out as couples. Acquaintances share statistics about kids' ages and skills and assume they've connected."[7]

Elisa Morgan makes a good point: Intimacy takes time. It takes commitment, not giving up easily, and believing in the other person. In our society it's easier to throw away than recycle, but recycling a friendship means searching for what's good and focusing on that.

Intimacy also means working to understand others and striving to be understood. It's not trying to change another person or having that person try to change you. Intimacy involves risk.

Intimacy Obstacle 1: Time and Energy

When it comes to friendships with other moms, the two most important ingredients for intimacy are time and energy, which are often in short supply.

With numerous responsibilities filling your day, often the last thing you have time for is girl time with friends. (And if by some crazy miracle you do have free time, often your first choice is sleep or laundry!)

"What I really wanted to talk about with other new moms were the things I didn't hear anyone really talking about. I wanted to know if mothering was difficult for them too, whether everyone else had the same doubts or if it was challenging only for me," says author Andrea J. Buchanan. "We talk about our babies' physical progress, how they are beginning to roll or starting to raise their heads. We talk about losing pregnancy weight. We talk about feeding and diapering. I am so hungry for contact with people who understand the daily routine of life with a new baby that this almost suffices."[8]

Sometimes moms are also too tired to set aside quality time with a husband or boyfriend. It seems the guy in our life is the last one in line to get attention (which is not a good thing when he is supposed to be your partner). Quality time with him can be, should be, spent in many different ways: having fun, talking, sharing dreams and values, and planning for the future.

My Life

Hugs and kisses are big in our home. I don't want our children growing up without affection. Whether it is story time, play time, or cuddle time, we find time to let each member of our little family know we love them. After all, children don't stay little forever.

— Marjie, Montana

Intimacy Obstacle 2: Finding (and Growing) Good Friends

Many young moms have a hard time transitioning between old friends and new ones. Friends their age are involved with teen stuff. Older moms are at a different stage in their lives, focusing on husbands, house payments, SUVs, and friends their own age.

I remember how uncomfortable I felt attending Lamaze classes during my pregnancy with my mother as my coach. Everyone else was with a spouse, and while they chatted about decorating nurseries and taking maternity leave, I felt left out.

It's a rare treasure to find someone who can understand your unique role as a young mom. Someone who is facing the same challenges and enjoys the same things.

For some of us the problem may not be finding good friends, but rather nurturing our good friendships to the next level. Have you taken time to understand someone for who they truly are, and not simply for who you wish them to be? Have others treated you the same?

Once you learn to accept each other, then it comes down to:

1. spending time with your friend,
2. listening,
3. helping your friend where she needs it,
4. and offering a glimpse of yourself in order to take your friendships to the next level.

Friendship is not just a one-way street. To grow a good friendship, you need to be willing to invest in it. Sometimes we feel so needy that all we think about is filling ourselves up, but in order to truly get, we need to give first.

Take a few minutes to think about your friends. What could you give that would make a difference? How do you think it would help?

Also, because your life has changed, you may be worried that you don't know how to connect with your friends like you used to. Remember, just because your friendship is different doesn't mean that it's wrong. When you value the people around you, something good will come out of it, even if it doesn't look the same as it used to.

It's hard enough to find good friends; it's important to keep them. Finding a good boyfriend is even harder, and sometimes that means letting go of the one you already have.

Intimacy Obstacle 3: Finding a Good Boyfriend

When looking for a good boyfriend, the emphasis must be on *good*. This can be a problem for those who have a habit of falling into unhealthy relationships.

We lose our objectivity in picking a boyfriend for different reasons. One reason is that we're needy. We need someone to like us, and if he is breathing, that's good enough.

Then there's the fear factor. Afraid of being alone, we wonder, *What if this is the only person who will love me?*

Fear plays a part, especially when we're looking for a relationship with a guy. The guys who are most interested in us often don't have the best reputations, but we're desperate to be loved, so we fall for them. We look past all the warning signs and tell ourselves that they'll change. (Note to self: they rarely change.)

Another reason we may not choose a good, dependable boyfriend is that we have no idea what a healthy relationship looks like. Perhaps you've had negative role models, and you find yourself picking the same type of creepy guys or codependent friends that your mom or sister had. For many moms this is the case.

I remember one specific meeting at our teen moms support group. I'd brought in three happily married couples to talk about marriage. I expected the young moms to ask questions about how to find the right person or how to deal with conflict, but that is not what they asked. Instead, the same question kept popping up over and over again, "Why in the world would you get married?"

The young women were happy for the couples—they really were—but they had no intention of getting married themselves. I was in shock. Then I began asking questions.

First of all, I asked how many of them had parents who were currently married. *None* of them. Not one of the young women raised her hand. Then I asked these young women how many of their parents had at one time been married to each other. Out of twenty-five young women, only two of them had parents who'd been married, but both were now divorced. I then asked how many of them had a good relationship with their father. Again, only two young women. Finally, I asked if any of them had ever *seen* a good marriage close up, one they'd like to model in their own lives. Out of twenty-five young moms, only one person raised her hand.

No wonder these young women had no hopes of marriage in the future. No wonder they were building relationships with the wrong types of guys. They had no idea what a happy marriage looks like. They had no idea what to hold out for.

Maybe you're the same. You like the idea of marriage and of a happy relationship, but you haven't had a good example in your life. You think pursuing such a thing is a waste of time, so you settle for far, far less. I'm here to tell you that it is possible. Once I started looking for—and praying for—the right type of guy, I found him. (As I mentioned before, I also changed my life to become the type of person the right type of guy would want.)

You have to start by being willing to wait for the right person, being willing to change, and being willing to open your heart when the time comes. It's time to break the cycle of bad relationships. How?

1. One way may be to step back from your romantic relationship for a moment and take a closer look. Is your boyfriend trustworthy? Is he loving? If your best friend were dating someone exactly like him, would you approve?
2. Ask yourself why you choose the type of men you do. Is it because of the examples of others? Is it because you don't think you can get anyone better? Is it because that is the type of person your mom dates and you don't know any better?
3. If you were able to do it all over, would you choose this person (either boyfriend or friend) to be in your life today? If not, why are you choosing to keep this person?

One thing I often ask teen moms is, "Is this man a good role model for your son? Would you want your son to grow up to be just like him?" The answer is usually no.

Or, "Is this the type of guy you want your baby girl to pick when she grows up? If your daughter was dating a guy just like this, would you approve?" Again, the answer is usually no.

I know it may be difficult. Evaluating your relationships may mean taking risks and stepping outside your insecurities. Remember, you are the example now. The positive relationships you model will make a huge difference in the type of people your child will choose. It'll be hard to break off an unhealthy relationship, but the longer it takes, the harder it will be!

Or maybe you're in a season of life when you just need a break from dating. That's okay too! Some single moms strive to better themselves and grow into their new role without having a boyfriend. It gives them more time to focus on their growth and who they want to be.

If you focus on becoming a whole person, then you'll be ready for the right guy, and often he'll find you. It's okay to not want to focus on a guy in your life. Instead, strive to make the right decisions, Mom, despite your fear of being alone. Know that when you make positive changes, the right person will come at the right time. Sometimes you have to be willing to let go of the frog in order to find the prince.

Intimacy Obstacle 4: Realizing You Are Worthy of a Loving, Committed Partner

"I'll never have any suitors," said Meg.

"You don't need scores of suitors. Only one, if he is the right one,"
answered Amy, setting her straight.

— From *Little Women* by Louisa May Alcott

What qualities were you looking for when you hooked up with your baby daddy? Was he the guy you always dreamed of?

I have a friend, Lynette, who made a list of all the qualities she was looking for in a husband. Some of the things she included in her list were confidence, kindness, and a tender heart. She was also looking for someone who would be her best friend, laugh easily, and treat her like a lady. Lynette set her standards high. Because she was looking with those things in mind, she found (and married) that type of guy.

I know of someone else who also had high standards for her future mate. A young woman named Ruth once wrote in her diary, "If I marry, he must be so tall that when he is on his knees, he reaches all the way to heaven. His lips must be broad enough to bear a smile, firm enough to say no, and tender enough to kiss. He must be big enough to be gentle and great enough to be thoughtful. His arms must be strong enough to carry a little child."[9]

The author of these words was Ruth Bell Graham, the wife of the most famous evangelist of all time, Billy Graham. And while no relationship is ever perfect (even this one), setting your standards high will bring a person into your life you can live with and love for a lifetime.

When I hear stories like Lynette's and Ruth's, I think, *If only I had the wisdom of these ladies!* In high school, I admit my top two criteria were: (1) good looks, and (2) thinks I look good. Having higher standards would have saved me a lot of heartache.

What qualities are you looking for? What would you place on your list?

Another question to ask is, What qualities do *you* have to offer?

We all want a great guy, but do we have the qualities to attract one? If not, which qualities do you need to work on? What is one thing that you can focus on that will make you the right type of partner?

Of course, sometimes it's hard to realize that you are worthy of a loving, committed partner. It's also hard to stop and consider what type of partner is best for you, especially when the world places more emphasis on looks than on heart.

My Life

I have a husband, but he doesn't make me feel any less lonely. I wish he would spend more time with me.

— Amanda, *Ontario, Canada*

I haven't had a boyfriend since I found out I was pregnant. I am a lot closer to my friends now because the ones I have accept me as a mother.

— Jamie, *Montana*

Where to Find Intimacy

The first duty of love is to listen.

— Paul Tillich, *theologian*

We know now that intimacy is connecting on different levels with good friends or a good partner. Still, where do we find it? Intimacy can happen in a park as you talk with a friend. It can happen in your marriage or committed relationship when you take time to listen to and respect each other. It can also happen in a support group such as Teen MOPS where you meet with other like-minded moms.

One relationship that isn't designed to meet your need for intimacy is the one you have with your child. Our children will always be a part of our hearts, but they are not there to meet our needs. I've often heard young moms say that they decided to have a child so they'd have "someone to love me." Children do love you (most of the time), but they shouldn't have to grow up under the pressure of making you happy.

Marriage

If you are married, your husband should be your main source of intimacy. Of course, even married partners have different views of what intimacy means. One partner might think of intimacy as physical closeness (such as sex), while the other partner thinks of intimacy as being understood. In another case, one partner might show love by buying gifts, while the other person shows love by washing the dishes.

It's important to express love to our spouse in a way he understands. Sit down with your partner in a quiet place and finish these sentences.

1. I feel loved when you …
2. One thing you did this week that made me feel loved is …

You may be surprised by the answers!

Making Time for Each Other

Married couples often feel they are heading in opposite directions, especially if they have different work and school schedules. In our home, my husband heads to work at 7:30 every morning, and I work from home. While I'm always eager to get busy on the computer, I find the mornings before he leaves are a good time for connecting. We talk as we eat our cereal. (What? Did you expect me to cook breakfast?) We also pray a one-minute prayer together, and I wave from the window when he drives away.

It sounds like the perfect arrangement, right? Let me assure you, this has been a work in progress. It all started when I took the time to think of one thing I could do to make time for my husband. (Getting out of bed was a good start.) Then, each of these other things was added over time.

Here are some other things we do.

- *Greet each other.* Whenever one of us arrives home, we take time to kiss and catch up about the day's events.
- *Have movie time after the kids go to bed.* It's great to snuggle on the couch together.
- *Go to bed at the same time.* I'm an early person and my husband is a night owl. We compromise by going to bed together about 10:30 p.m. (This is when the next level of intimacy begins!)

Unrealistic Expectations

If two words ever hurt intimacy, they are *unrealistic expectations*. I'll be the first to admit that this was my major struggle when we got married!

As you know, I had some bad relationships in the past, so when I found John, who was loving, dedicated, trustworthy, and handsome, I thought I'd found the perfect guy. We had a quick engagement, and we were married nine months after our first date!

While dating, John and I spent a lot of time talking, so I thought I knew him pretty well. I also saw what kind of lifestyle he led. John worked hard at his job and at home. His house was always neat, and he even ironed his own clothes. (See why I thought he was perfect?)

Needless to say, when we got married, I had unrealistic expectations. We'd never talked about it, but I assumed that since he always cleaned and did laundry for himself, he would do it for all of us.

Wrong!

And that was only one of our issues. I could spend all day discussing conflicts like where to go at Christmas, how to spend money, how to discipline our kids — the list is long.

But in the end, it all comes down to communication and compromise. Years later, we still work on these things. I have my opinion. He has his. But talking through our issues, without getting upset, has helped us to unite in our marriage. It has also fostered our intimacy, because the more time we spend talking through problems and coming to compromises, the closer we become. And isn't that what intimacy is all about?

Dear Friend,

I've been wanting to write this letter for a while. It took me a while to get up the nerve. I care for you, you see. But I want to make sure you're willing to listen. I want you to know that I'm saying these things because I care for you, not because I have a point to prove.

Listen to me when I tell you that from this point on you can make the decision not to be sexually active until marriage. I don't care what the world has told you. I don't care what you see on TV. I don't care what your friends are doing. I care about you. You.

I care about you and the way you are treating yourself. You are beautiful and special, and yet you treat yourself as if you have nothing special to give — or to save.

I'm not sure why you became sexually active in the first place. Was it because for the first time someone noticed you and made you feel beautiful? (That was my reason.)

Was it because your innocence was taken away from you before you understood what was happening? You never had a chance to make a choice about sex; the choice was just forced on you.

Did you have sex because you were curious about it? Did you wonder how it would feel — during and after?

Did you think you'd feel more grown up?

Did you think it was too long to wait until marriage? Did you wonder if marriage was even worth it?

Did you think he'd love you?

Did you think he'd stay around?

Did you hope it would be the start of something wonderful?

Something good happened. You're a mom now. But as wonderful as your child is, there are a whole lot of issues that have resulted in you having sex outside of the commitment of marriage.

He didn't stay. Or if he did, you worry he won't always.

You feel more grown up in a way, but there are days you wish you didn't have all the responsibility.

There is the STD issue. Yeah, you know what I'm talking about. More teens today have an STD than don't, and it affects everything.

There is also your heart. You've felt a sweep of emotions — the highs and the lows. You never thought you'd feel so loved, and you never dreamed you'd be so hurt.

The truth is that God created us — men and women — to be bonded to one person for life. When we give ourselves, we give everything, and each time after we have less to give.

You feel different from the way you used to, and things will never be the same. But there is one change you can make that will make all the difference. Stop having sex.

If you're worried he'll leave, well, he might. But do you really want someone hanging around who is interested only in your body, not your heart and your soul?

If he does love you, he will want to honor you. He <u>will</u> stick around. Then you can do this thing the right way. You can seek God together, get married, and start a life you can be proud of. It won't be easy, but it'll be right.

When you protect your body, you're protecting your heart and soul. You're putting value on <u>you</u>. You're also becoming a good example for your child.

How do you want your child to live? Live that way, and you'll begin training your child for life.

I want to tell you something else: God is here to help you. He's not going to condemn you. He's not a big bully who just wants you to do things his way.

He loves you more than you can imagine. He has dreams for you. He created you, and he has a good plan for you. When the rest of the world has <u>their</u> agenda, and wants to use you for what <u>they</u> can get, God has your best interests at heart. He has rules because he knows that when you follow them, you'll find more joy and peace than you ever experienced. I promise you that.

Pray to Jesus and ask him to help you. Ask him to keep you strong. Ask Jesus to bring someone into your life who will love you for <u>you</u>, and not just your body. Ask Jesus to bring you someone who loves your child as his own.

What's the worst that can happen? You might not date certain guys. You might have to put limits on where you go and what you do. You might be teased.

<u>What's the benefit?</u> You'll respect yourself. Your child will respect you. You'll be a good example. You'll also have the chance to draw near to God and allow him to impact your life. I guarantee you won't regret it.

A fresh start is something beautiful. You are worthy of this, friend.

You are worthy.

A Craving for Belonging

We're all lonely for something we don't know we're lonely for. How else to explain the curious feeling that goes around like missing somebody we've never even met?

— David Foster Wallace, *novelist*

I remember the last few days of my pregnancy. I was lonely and bored.

When I mentioned my boredom to a friend who had kids, she laughed. "Once you become a mom, that will change," she said. "You may have days when you'll be lonely, but you'll never be bored."

I soon discovered my friend was right. In my new role as a mother, there was no time to be bored. But loneliness was served up in abundance, along with a side dish of isolation.

Have you ever felt like something was missing? Or someone? A heart friend. A partner. Someone who would listen to your dreams, your troubles, and even that day-to-day stuff that comes up in your role as a mother.

Feelings of isolation and loneliness are among the biggest complaints from young moms. Overnight, they go from having lives filled with all types of people — parents, friends, teachers, coaches — to the monotony of having only one companion all day. As much as you love your little one, the shock of not having adults to talk to for hours at a time can be overwhelming. You miss your friends, but you feel different from them. More relationships don't work out than do. You want to be responsible, but that means turning your back on people and situations that aren't good for your child. Sometimes being responsible is a lonely place to be.

As a young mom-to-be's abdomen swells, her list of friends usually shrinks. Sometimes it's due to changing roles. Other times it's due to changing hearts. Life is altered. We don't connect as easily. We can't do the same things. And no matter how much we tell ourselves that this baby will not change us, we feel different inside.

Yet, as with every other person, we are born with an inward need to connect. Babies in crowded orphanages lose brain function from lack of touch.[10] When we don't connect with others who love us, something inside of us dies too.

I know one young mom who was scorned by her family when she became pregnant. Her parents allowed her to live with them but offered little love or support. Her life became a series of disconnections—chores, caring for baby, work. Even though her boyfriend was physically abusive, she moved in with him. She was desperately unhappy, but to her, the rocky relationship was better than isolation. And she's still in that difficult relationship to this day. This young mom needed to feel loved—at any cost.

We all do. It's how we were created.

The Bible discusses this human need within its first few pages. In Genesis, it talks about God filling the earth with an abundance of life: animals, birds, and fish. And it was good. Yet the man God created, Adam, was alone. And that was not good.

My Life

No female wants to be the "baby's mama." People need to stop thinking it's cute and fun to be a single mom at a young age! I swear to you, it's hard. It's giving away freedom, time, money. You'll be pushed past your limit! You'll lose a lot. You'll break down. You'll feel the real struggle! I wish someone would have sat me down and told me the raw truth of being a parent!! I love my kids a lot! I do, but I have to struggle to provide for them, and my ex of five years just sees me as just the baby's mama! Not what I wanted for my kids, for me, or for him!

— Elizabeth, *Arkansas*

I feel the most lonely after I put my baby down for the night. I don't have him to grin at me. Sometimes it feels like I'm the only one in the world who's awake at 9 p.m.

— Amanda, *Ontario, Canada*

That's where Eve came in. She was a special creation, designed to meet a specific need. Eve was someone Adam could talk with, work with, live with, and love. But that's not the only place the Bible talks about the importance of a companion. Ecclesiastes 4:9–12 (LB) says: "Two can accomplish more than twice as much as one, for the results can be much better. If one falls, the other pulls him up; but if a man falls when he is alone, he's in trouble. Also, on a cold night, two under the same blanket gain warmth from each other, but how can one be warm alone? And one standing alone can be attacked and defeated, but two can stand back-to-back and conquer."

God knows all about this thing called loneliness. He created us to connect with others. He created us with the need to love and be loved.

Unfortunately, loneliness can be more of a problem for young mothers than it is for older moms. Young moms often feel isolated from their friends, who are busy with normal teen activities: school, sports, or hanging out. And often, with all the many changes, young moms have little energy or opportunity for new relationships with people who understand being a mom and a teen. The thing is, if you don't fill that emptiness in your heart with positive relationships, you'll soon let your guard down and allow negative ones in. It just works that way. So what to do? Here are some ways to connect:

Everyone Needs a Friend

I can relate to feeling lonely. I remember sitting, bored, as I watched my son play on the lawn in front of our apartment complex. As I looked at the puffy white clouds that graced the summer sky, I thought of the days when my friend Dawn and I used to just hang out at the lake and talk. Lying on our backs, we'd whisper and laugh. We'd flip to our stomachs and read magazines, pointing out cute outfits and hairstyles. But we were older now, and we lived miles apart. I missed her, and I wondered if I'd ever have another friend like that.

Just then another young mom walked by with her daughter. I dared to call a hello. She smiled and approached. Our kids played together that day and many days to follow. I'd found a new friend.

Making friends means reaching out. Here are places to start:

- Neighborhood parks
- Fitness clubs, which sometimes have classes for mothers and their children (The YMCA offers "well-baby" classes at a low cost.)
- Coffee shops where mothers gather
- Bike paths where energetic moms can push strollers
- Libraries that offer a story hour
- Churches. This is one of the best places to find moms. Many churches have programs targeted for young mothers, such as MOPS (Mothers of Preschoolers), often with free child care too! If there isn't a MOPS group near you, look around for other clubs for moms.

Once you find friends, then it's time to nurture those relationships. But before we talk about how to foster intimacy, let's define intimacy in various relationships.

To Have a Friend, Be a Friend

When you dream alone, with your eyes shut, asleep, that dream is an illusion. But when we dream together, sharing the same dream, awake and with our eyes wide open, then that dream becomes reality!

—Anonymous

Do you remember your first best friend? Mine was Heather. We attended church together and played during the week. Heather's mom worked in a furniture store, and we would play "orphanage," pretending to lay imaginary children down for naps in the display beds.

As Heather and I got older, we attended different schools and went our separate ways. Partings are a way of life. As each of us grows, we learn to appreciate more fully the various friends who cross our paths.

"Not every friend is meant to be our best friend," say Elisa Morgan and Carol Kuykendall, "and not every friendship is meant to be forever."[11] Still, each of us hopes to find a friend who will be just that.

Here are five things to look for in a friend. Can you think of five more?

1. Trust
2. Honesty
3. Common interests
4. A positive outlook
5. A sense of humor
6. _____
7. _____
8. _____
9. _____
10. _____

One final thing to remember is that even with all your friendships combined, people cannot be expected to meet every need. Just as God created the first man and woman with a need for each other, he also created them with a need for himself.

Theologian Henri Nouwen once wrote, "No friend or lover, no husband or wife, no community or commune will be able to put to rest our deepest cravings for unity and wholeness."

Some people may consider God as a far-off ruler who put people on this world, then left them to their own devices. This couldn't be farther from the truth. My favorite Scripture verse is Zephaniah 3:17 (NIV 1984), "The LORD your God is with you, he is mighty to save. He will take great delight in you, he will quiet you with his love, he will rejoice over you with singing."

I love this verse because it speaks of a God who is near. Who likes me. Who is able to calm me when I'm afraid. Who sings over me from his place in heaven. Now that's a friend I can appreciate!

Let's Talk about It

Springboards to Deeper Conversation

Do you want to get to know a new friend better, but you don't know where to start? Here are some conversation starters.

1. What is the happiest thing that has ever happened to you?
2. What has been the hardest experience of your life?
3. What are your secret ambitions, your goals for your life?
4. What are your deepest fears?
5. What about me do you appreciate the most?
6. What people do you most admire?[12]

Hello, Mr. Right

Eighteen Attributes to Look for in a Marriage Partner

Looking for Mr. Right? Think about the qualities you desire in a mate. Write them down. Here are a few to get you started.

1. Positive attitude
2. Spiritual values
3. Sense of humor
4. Faithfulness
5. Honesty
6. Respect
7. Good communication skills
8. Hard worker
9. Compassionate
10. Playful
11. Generous
12. Forgiving
13. Flexible
14. Confident
15. Sensitive
16. Understanding
17. Uses common sense
18. Wise with money

— Al Gray and Alice Gray, in *Lists to Live By for Everything That Really Matters*[13]

Live and Learn

I was created to love and be loved.

5

How Do I Do This Mom Thing?

Instruction

Motherhood is like Albania — you can't trust the descriptions in the books, you have to go there.

— Marni Jackson, *The Mother Zone*

My baby wasn't feeling well at all. Cory was only four months old and I knew something wasn't right. He wasn't nursing. He was fussy. He was limp when I held him. I took him to the doctor, and the doctor told me that he only had colic. The doctor was in and out of the room in less than three minutes.

The next day Cory's fever was up to 103 degrees. He hadn't had a wet diaper in hours and hours. I called the emergency room. "Do you think I should bring him in?"

"Yes, of course!" The nurse seemed shocked that I had to ask. Once I got to the ER, they whisked him away. Cory was so dehydrated that they had to put a shunt into his leg to give him fluids. They quickly determined he had spinal meningitis, and they flew him, by a hospital plane, to a children's hospital. I was right there with him.

I was barely eighteen and a long way from home. The doctors and nurses looked to me to make decisions. I hadn't even voted yet, and here I was making life-and-death decisions for my child! Nothing had prepared me for this.

Thankfully Cory was fine. With the care of doctors and nurses—and a lot of prayer—he was released from the hospital four days later and made a complete recovery, but I soon realized that it was only the beginning of needing to be the one who had all the answers. As Cory grew older, the need for answers increased:

- how to discipline
- how to teach kindness
- when to set bedtime
- how to potty train
- whether or not to put him in preschool

My son didn't come with a manual, and it wasn't always easy to know the right answers. Over time I learned how to stand up for my son. I also figured out where to go for advice.

I learned how to do this mom thing one small decision after another. Thankfully I didn't have to do it alone.

What's a Mother to Do?

Your teen years have been filled with learning and test taking. Your history teacher lectured on the American Revolution, and then you were tested on dates and facts. To get your driver's license, you learned the rules of the road and then took a driving test. But when it comes to this motherhood thing, there are no lectures (except, perhaps, from your mom). There's no instructor in your passenger seat, making sure you follow the rules of the road.

"People said to me when I was pregnant, 'Oh, your life is going to change!' as if they were not stating the obvious. My life had already changed—I was pregnant," says Andrea J. Buchanan, author of *Mother Shock*. "I knew to expect sleepless nights; I knew to expect crying; I knew to expect exhaustion; I even knew to expect joy…. I didn't know to expect doubt."[1]

Mothers-to-be and new moms often overflow with doubt and questions. There's so much to learn about babies. There's the basic stuff, such as feeding, burping, and when to introduce solid foods. But beyond the early survival skills, there are new questions that arise daily in the early months. How do I get my child to sleep through the night, to stop throwing his food on the floor, to behave, to say please instead of demand?

Whether you're still tackling the basic skills of mothering or seeking advice on bigger issues, such as growth, personality, and development, the questions never end. So where can mothers turn for instruction?

Basic Instincts

Suddenly I was in unfamiliar territory. I'd had nine months to anticipate being a mother, and then about thirty seconds to snap into being one.

— Andrea J. Buchanan, *Mother Shock*

I remember those first few moments after my son was born. He was slimy, pink, and beautiful. I instinctively reached for him and held him to my chest, wanting nothing more than to give this child everything.

The mothering instinct is something that may surprise a new mom, especially one who hasn't had much experience with babies. Sometimes the mothering instinct kicks in from the start, and you know what your baby's cry means, or something tells you to seek a second opinion concerning your child's health. The mothering instinct is an inner nudge that won't go away.

But the mothering instinct shouldn't be thought of as some big, mystical change that transforms you the moment you give birth. Instead, it's more like a natural tendency to love and protect your child.

"Tough to prove and easy to dismiss ... maternal instinct is a place where a mom must learn to trust her heart in response to her child," says Elisa Morgan, author of *What Every Mom Needs*.

My Life

What I do is important. I am raising a child that one day will have to make decisions on his own, choices on his own, and know the difference from what is right and wrong. I want him to be a decent human being. I don't want to judge people by their looks, the way they act, etc. That in itself is extremely important because we need less ignorant people in the world. To me, my son is what he sees, so I make sure I am a very positive influence in his life.

— Diana, *Washington*

That's not to say that every mom has a mothering instinct. For some women it takes a while for them to "feel" like a mom. It's easy for them to let their mom, grandma, or auntie care for their child—after all, those older women know better (or so they think!). If you don't feel as if you have a mothering instinct, the best thing to do is to spend time with your child. Hold her, feed her, interact with her, watch her sleep, marvel over her fingers and toes. It's okay if it takes time to figure out the best way to hold and feed your baby. It's okay if you have to ask for advice on giving your baby a bath. What might not be there in natural instinct will be made up for with the skills you learn. Don't give up. The bonds you make with your child will grow as he grows older. Without those initial bonds, it'll be harder and harder to make a connection as your child gets older.

While it's normal to experience some sadness after having a baby, some moms also suffer postpartum depression, which, without help, can make them consider running away or hurting their child—things they'd typically never dream of doing. If you feel depressed, have thoughts of suicide, or thoughts of harming yourself or your baby, put your baby down in a safe place and call your doctor immediately. Many, many women struggle with depression after giving birth, and your doctor can help. Be willing to seek advice and help from caring family members and friends, too, so you don't have to face your depression alone.

For many of us, when we see that squishy baby and breathe in that baby smell, we begin loving and nurturing in ways we never thought possible. Even someone who has never considered herself a "baby person" may find herself suddenly changed when dealing with her own child. This is a gift from God. Remember this. Also remember to trust your instincts. The more time you spend with your child, the more you'll understand his needs and be able to meet them. And with each need you meet, your bond as mother and child will grow.

Learning about Mothering

When love and skill work together, expect a masterpiece.
— John Ruskin, *artist*

A hundred years ago it was common for families to live near each other, with the older mothers training the younger ones. Today, families are often spread across the country. Even if they live close, experienced family members may be unable to provide hands-on help. That's why today's mothers look to different sources for advice, including parenting books, classes, and private Facebook groups— the new "community." Wherever you look for advice, it's helpful to focus on one issue at a time.

What do you need to know most urgently about your mothering today? Stephen Covey, in his book *Seven Habits of Highly Effective People*, believes that effective people "begin with the end in mind." They know where they're headed, so they "take care to get there." Do you have an end in mind when it comes to your most urgent needs?

Knowing your goal will help you know what type of advice to seek out. If your end is good health, you'll seek information on nutrition, sleep, and exercise. If your goal is "smarts," you'll incorporate reading aloud and other mind-stimulating activities. If your goal is a happy, peaceful toddler, you'll seek information on how to control your schedule and your temper, to applaud every success, and to have fun with your baby. (No small task!)

Pause for a few minutes and make a list of goals that you want to accomplish as a parent. What type of parent do you want to be? What type of childhood do you want your child to have? Then ask one final question: What do you need to do today to get there? Your answers will change everything in a positive way!

How to Become a Lifelong Learner

When I became a mom at seventeen, I didn't know a lot. I dropped out of high school my senior year and finished my high school credits at home. I grew up in a small town, and my graduating class was under forty students. I'd gone to school with most of those students since kindergarten. My world was pretty small.

After high school I met and married my husband, started college, and moved to a new town. I learned how to take care of a house, how to clean, how to cook. Each growth step was hard, and thankfully my family and friends were still close.

When John and I moved more than one hour away for him to go to college, I felt as if we had traveled to a different universe. I learned how to live in a new town and how to make new friends. I started a small business making hand-crafted teddy bears, so I learned how to be a business woman.

A year after we moved, I had another baby, so I learned how to care for multiple children. I realized I was more interested in writing than in making teddy bears, and so I started doing that.

Wanting to become a professional writer, I attended conferences and started learning about writing. With each step came changes, and looking back, I realize that my greatest asset was my ability to roll up my sleeves and try something new.

Every day we have a choice: to take a step to follow a dream or to stay stagnant and continue on as things are. I've grown and changed throughout the years because I hadn't been afraid to learn. The wisest man who ever lived once said, "Do yourself a favor and learn all you can; then remember what you learn and you will prosper" (Prov. 19:8 GNT). He knew what he was talking about!

Here are five simple steps to becoming a life-long learner.

> ## Richer Than Gold
>
> You may have tangible wealth untold;
> Caskets of jewels and coffers of gold.
> Richer than I you can never be —
> I had a mother who read to me.
>
> —Strickland Gillian (1849–1954)

1. *Learn who God created you to be.* Think about what things you enjoy doing. Make a list of things that take your time and energy but don't seem like work. For a season I enjoyed being creative and making teddy bears, but when I first started pursuing writing, I *knew* I was made for this. I find joy even in the middle of the struggle. I always want to know more and do better. Work doesn't seem like work (most of the time).

2. *Learn your learning style.* I learn best with books and papers piled around me. I usually have to write down my thoughts to process them. When I read a book, I underline. When I attend conferences, I take pages of notes, and that's just me. Figure out how you learn best and use your preferences to your advantage.

3. *Listen.* I've learned so much from listening to others. I build relationships with people I respect and want to learn from. I read blogs written by people I respect. I pay attention to those around me in everyday life.

4. *Don't be afraid to try something new.* I try new recipes and visit new places. I watch how-to videos and then try it myself.

5. *Teach.* The best way to incorporate your knowledge is to teach it. As a mom, you have a willing student in your child. Involve your child in whatever you're learning. If you're cooking, let your little one watch you. Your child should know the things that interest you.

Learning can take you far—you just have to be brave and start! Once you start learning and growing, your life will never be the same. Your child's life will never be the same either as he or she learns to follow in your footsteps!

Expert Advice

> *When I first became pregnant, I craved not only spicy chicken
> sandwiches and fries but also information. I realized that one Bible
> class and a childhood of eavesdropping on my mom and her friends
> wasn't going to cut it in terms of preparing me for the reality of
> childbirth and parenthood.*
>
> — Andrea J. Buchanan, *Mother Shock*

Where do you turn for good advice from trustworthy sources?

Doctors and nurses can be good resources. I know one young mom who was struggling to nurse her son. She thought she had to figure it out herself. She mentioned it in passing to her doctor, and the doctor sat down with her until she had the baby latched on and gulping. She's since learned that doctors and nurses are happy to help with almost any parenting question.

When you can't get in to see someone in person (such as over the weekend), you can seek out nurse hotlines. Check with your local hospital or insurance company to see if they offer this service.

Other good places to search for advice are magazines and books, or radio and television programs. Here are some pointers for knowing which resources to trust.

- *Shop around.* Just because someone has an MD or a PhD behind his name doesn't mean his advice is right for you.
- *Get referrals from friends.* If you see parents with well-behaved children, ask them for their favorite books and resources.
- *Consider more than one resource.* Read books and magazines and pick out what works for you. Choose the best and don't bother with the rest.
- *Consider your current needs.* As your child grows, your parenting style may need to change. What worked at twelve months may not work at twenty months.
- *Listen to your heart.* Remember that no one parenting style works for every person. What is your heart telling you?

- *Seek help before a bad habit forms.* Kids ages two years old and older know how to "work" Mommy. For instance, they'll throw a terrible tantrum in the store, knowing Mom has to give in. The next time that happens, how are you going to handle it? Ask knowledgeable mothers for the best way to deal with situations such as this.

Unsolicited Advice

Sometimes you look for advice, and, like it or not, at other times advice finds you. If you feed your baby a bottle, someone will advise you to breastfeed. If you breastfeed, you'll hear that your baby isn't getting enough milk, and you should offer a bottle. You'll hear well-meaning phrases like these:

- "Use disposable diapers."
- "Use cloth diapers."
- "Let him cry."
- "Pick him up."
- "Rock him."
- "Drive him around the block until he falls asleep."

The list is endless.

"Everyone, it seemed, had an opinion that I needed to hear, and often everyone's opinion was different," says Andrea Buchanan. "'Take it from me,' people would say. Or, 'Let me tell you,' they'd begin. Whatever they said would always end with some piece of vital information that would doom me to eternal bad parenthood if I ignored it."

There are a few things you can do when others insist on telling you what they think, including:

1. Ignoring it.
2. Appreciating it.
3. Getting irritated.

The best choice is a mix of numbers 1 and 2. Listen and be polite, but don't feel you have to follow their suggestions. (I agree that it's hard to do!)

Of course, when advice is given in a condemning way, it's challenging not to be annoyed. This usually doesn't even have anything to do with you; it has everything to do with the person giving the advice. Some people just like to be nosey or bossy. Many people are unhappy, and unkind words just seep out of them. Maybe deep down they wish they had a do-over, or they're feeling afraid or insecure in their own parenting choices. People are sometimes quick to stick labels on you and your child. But realize that in the end you're the parent, and what you think is what matters most.

It's also a good reminder to us. We can be the expert on our kids, but we should be diligent to give advice only when asked.

Moral Instruction

Another thing that kicks in when you become a mother is your natural tendency to share your values, faith, and beliefs with your child. Inner convictions help you determine how to treat others. Convictions also help with decision making.

Most of the time, the values you choose to communicate aren't something you sit around and think about. Instead of writing out a ten-step plan for how to teach love, you simply model it.

Some values you got from your parents. Others you've seen modeled in people you respect. Just like scanning papers into your computer, moms soon discover their kids often turn out to be miniature copies of themselves.

"Children are natural observers," says Emilie Barnes, author of *Time Began in a Garden*. "In fact, I've found that children see so much more than adults do, perhaps because they're closer to the ground, perhaps because they look at the world through fresh eyes."

So what qualities do you want your child to pick up? Do you want her to know she shouldn't judge people by their outward appearance? Do you want her to be respectful of other people's things and ideas? Do you long for her to eat nutritiously and exercise, or love to read, or keep a clean room? Then you must show her how it's done. Modeling these behaviors is a gift to your child.

This is also a time to start considering what behaviors you need to change. Do you have any bad habits? Know that your child will pick them up quickly! Work on the things that you want to change, not only for yourself but also for your child. And don't feel that you have to do it alone. Ask a friend to keep you accountable. Reward yourself for small changes made. Also, pray to God and ask for his help. He wants you to come to him—not because he's focused on you becoming a perfect mom or perfect person (no one is), but God wants you to come to him so your relationship will grow. He wants to help you, but he wants to spend life with you even more.

"Do as I Do"

Want to know something that's impossible? Sneezing with your eyes open. Something else that is impossible is raising a child under the concept, "Do as I say, not as I do."

For myself, I want my children to know God's love and to know that he speaks to us through the Bible. So from the time they were very young, I've made prayer and Bible reading a part of our everyday lives.

Some people think reading the Bible is a good idea, but they have no idea where to start. The most important place to start is by reading the four sections (books) labeled Matthew, Mark, Luke, and John. These four books talk about Jesus. They are compiled from eye-witness accounts of his time on earth.

Jesus is the center of the Bible. Everything leading up to Matthew, Mark, Luke, and John is information about people and their need for God. Everything after Matthew, Mark, Luke, and John are writings from Jesus' followers who wrote about how to apply Jesus' teaching to everyday life.

You don't have to change before you read the Bible, but if you read the Bible with an open heart, you might soon start wanting to

Qualities to Pass On to Your Children

- Determination: "Stick with it, regardless."
- Honesty: "Speak and live the truth — always."
- Responsibility: "Be dependable, be trustworthy."
- Thoughtfulness: "Think of others before yourself."
- Confidentiality: "Don't tell secrets. Seal your lips."
- Punctuality: "Be on time."
- Self-control: "When under stress, stay calm."
- Patience: "Fight irritability. Be willing to wait."
- Purity: "Reject anything that lowers your standards."
- Compassion: "When another hurts, feel it with him."
- Diligence: "Work hard. Tough it out."

—Charles R. Swindoll, author of *Growing Strong in the Seasons of Life*[2]

change. When you read the Bible, you will see that Jesus was wonderful at giving instruction. He didn't do it by giving lists of rules. Instead, he did it by caring for people. He loved hanging out with people the world looked down upon. Jesus was the hardest on the religious people—those who acted like they did everything right. Don't believe me? Read Matthew, Mark, Luke, and John and discover this for yourself.

Know that if Jesus were on earth today, he wouldn't look down on you. Instead, he'd love hanging out with you. He'd love sharing what's on his heart, hoping you'd pass it on.

Knowing what's important to Jesus will help determine what things to pass on to your children. And as you read the Bible your convictions may change. When change comes, it's important to be true to your convictions even when it is difficult or inconvenient. It means not settling with what's easy, and instead pursuing what's right. Just like Jesus did. He loved telling his followers, "Do what I do." And as you follow Jesus, you can say the same thing to your child with confidence.

Mothering Mentors

No one is a light unto themselves, not even the sun.

— Antonio Porchia, *author*

Have you ever met a person and thought, *I want to be like that when I grow up?* When I first became a mother, I looked to a woman named Cheryl as an example. She was caring and spoke to her children with affection. She smiled often and didn't get upset easily.

Everyone needs someone to look up to. I've had women in my life whom I esteemed as mentors, whether they knew it or not. In fact, I'm not sure if Cheryl even realized she was "mentoring" me. She was a young, married mom of two children, and I met her when I returned to church. We'd often talk about parenting, and sometimes I'd ask advice. More often than not I'd just watch how she guided her kids, how she praised them, and how she encouraged their efforts. Her gentle spirit was an inspiration to me, and I worked hard to be a mother like that. Cheryl made a difference in my life even when she didn't realize it.

How about you? Do you have someone you can follow, someone who is a great mom? You can watch her, or you can ask her to mentor you. Many women are honored to be asked.

Finding a Mentor

There are various places to find mentors. Some moms find them when they join play groups or support groups. Others look in places of worship to find women of common interests or cultural backgrounds.

A mentor is someone who has been where you are going. She's faced the same struggles, experienced the same joys, and usually has good advice.

Mentoring is not a new concept. Even the Bible talks about this type of relationship. Titus 2:4–5 (MSG) says, "By looking at [older women], the younger women will know how to love their husband and children, be virtuous and pure, keep a good house, be good wives."

Many times mentoring also moves past the outward stuff and unites hearts. And while it may seem like the younger mother reaps all the benefits, older mentors greatly enjoy the relationship too. So when you spot someone who may fit the role, don't be afraid to ask her to be your mentor. Invite her to meet you for coffee, and use the opportunity to listen to her stories and enjoy her company. She'll appreciate getting to know you in an intimate way and will cherish the joy of helping, as perhaps she was once helped too.

When you look for a female mentor, ask yourself the following questions:

- Who do I admire? Do I have an older friend, relative, or perhaps a leader in a Teen MOPS group I'd enjoy spending more time with?
- Does this person have time to spend with me?
- What can this person teach me about life? Parenting? Following dreams? Will this person encourage my growth?
- Is this person a healthy role model? Is she honest? Truthful? Accepting? Supportive?
- Does this person take time to listen to my concerns? Can I open up to this person? Can this person be trusted with my confidence?

If you find someone, here are steps to setting up a mentoring relationship:

- Ask if she'd be interested in becoming a mentor.
- State what you're looking for.
- Take time to interact, to listen, and to care.
- Give as well as receive.

Once you find someone to build a relationship with, together you can decide on the specifics of your time together. It's up to each individual mentoring relationship to consider their needs and goals. Consider:

- How often do you want to meet?
- What types of things would each of you like to discuss?

- What level of commitment are you willing to give?
- What will you do when you meet? Talk and share feelings, hopes, and dreams? Go through a book together? Pray?

Peers

Since not everyone has a mentor in their lives, the most common place that mothers, young and old, get advice is from their friends. Moms ask questions and swap advice through text messages, Facebook, short discussions in the grocery store, during work, or at play time.

For a more focused arrangement, try looking for support and encouragement through a Teen MOPS group. To see if there is Teen MOPS in your area, check out *www.mops.org*.

Other places to call are local hospitals, churches, or parenting organizations in your community. We all need someone who understands. Nothing feels better than to share your up-all-night-baby-wouldn't-stop-crying experience with someone who can sympathize.

My Life

I can only do what I can. There will be times I'll be discouraged, but with my determination and personality I know I'll make it. I just want to be a good mother, and wife, and that'll take a lot of effort and work. Right now, I've just been looking at other mothers, reading books, talking to family, and getting as much "guidance" as I can.

— Katherine, *Texas*

Jesus, the Instructor

Still, there are times when not even peers are available. That's why it's good to know that there is one person who's always available. Jesus is not only there to listen, he's there to instruct you with his words of truth. Still wondering what to do, where to go, how to live?

"Let God transform you inwardly by a complete change of mind. Then you will be able to know the will of God—what is good and is pleasing to him and is perfect" Romans 12:2 (GNT).

And isn't that the exact type of instruction we're looking for—instruction that is complete, good, pleasing, and perfect? For that, go to Jesus.

Good Things to Say

Wise Things Your Grandma Told You

Model these concepts for your child!

- You are special.
- Manners matter.
- Treat others the way you want to be treated.
- Your life can be what you want it to be.
- Take the days one day at a time.
- Always play fair.
- Count your blessings, not your troubles.
- Don't put limits on yourself.
- It's never too late.
- Put things back where you found them.
- Decisions are too important to leave to chance.
- Reach for the stars.
- Clean up after yourself.
- Nothing wastes more energy than worrying.
- The longer you carry a problem, the heavier it gets.
- Say "I'm sorry" when you've hurt someone.
- A little love goes a long way.
- Friendship is always a good investment.
- Don't take things too seriously.[3]

Wise Sayings to Remember

There's been much good instruction passed down through the ages. Here are some keepers from *The Message*, in the book of Proverbs.

- "Better a bread crust shared in love than a slab of prime rib served in hate" (Prov. 15:17).
- "Hot tempers start fights; a calm, cool spirit keeps the peace" (Prov. 15:18).
- "Refuse good advice and watch your plans fail; take good counsel and watch them succeed" (Prov. 15:22).
- "Put God in charge of your work, then what you've planned will take place" (Prov. 16:3).
- "Friends love through all kinds of weather, and families stick together in all kinds of trouble" (Prov. 17:17).
- "Answering before listening is both stupid and rude" (Prov. 18:13).
- "Trust God from the bottom of your heart; don't try to figure out everything on your own" (Prov. 3:5).
- "Listen for God's voice in everything you do, everywhere you go; he's the one who will keep you on track" (Prov. 3:6).

Things Kids Say

Helpful Advice

Are you tired of getting advice you didn't ask for? Here's some you might appreciate. In his book *Never Eat Anything That Moves*, Robert Bender gleaned the following advice from children. Here are some of my favorites:

- "Never pull a cat's tail or the other end will bite you" (Brigham Shipley, age 10).
- "If you can't find your gum, your shoe will find it for you" (Joslyn Smeal, age 11).
- "One best friend is worth one hundred lukewarm ones" (Joseph Hyde, age 10).

- "The worst advice I ever gave was when my brother asked me if B comes before A" (I told him yes, but I wasn't paying attention. When he sang his BACs, it sounded awful" (Desi Casada, age 8).
- "You're not in school to make friends. That's what detention is for" (Adriano Apostolico, age 12).
- "If you get a bad grade on a test, tell your mom when she's on the phone" (Nichole Murphy, age 11).
- "Never pick your nose when your mom slams on the brakes" (Lacey Shaffer, age 10).
- "When you get mad, don't let your pain stay inside, you might break down" (Brittney Robinson, age 11).
- "To sing louder, open your mouth and pretend there's an Oreo in it" (Dianna Vo, age 11).
- "It's good to be young, because you will last longer" (Cara Iglady, age 7).[4]

Repeat After Me

Instructions to think about and live for:

- The six most important words: "I admit I made a mistake."
- The five most important words: "You did a good job."
- The four most important words: "What is your opinion?"
- The three most important words: "If you please."
- The two most important words: "Thank you."
- The one most important word: "We."
- The least important word: "I."[5]

Try This

My Personal Favorite Advice

- If you tell your child to do something, follow through.
- Teach your child to obey the first time.
- Don't let your child do at six months what you don't want her to do at two years. Sticking his tongue out or saying bad words may be cute with a baby, but it doesn't stay cute.
- Don't let your baby use items as toys, such as phones or keys, that you wouldn't want them to play with when they get older.
- Don't teach your baby words that you'd hate for them to repeat in public. Swear words might sound cute coming from the mouth of a toddler, but they aren't cute coming from the mouth of a four-year-old.

Live and Learn

Seeking information helps me to become an informed mom.

6

Can You Help?

Help

There is no such thing as a self-made man. You will reach your goals only with the help of others.

— George Shinn, *owner of the New Orleans Hornets*

Becoming a first-time mom at such a young age was hard, but things started off well at first. I was able to breastfeed Cory and he slept fine—as well as could be expected for a newborn baby. We seemed to be getting into a good routine, but when he was around three weeks old, Cory woke up in the middle of the night with a cry I hadn't heard before. I tried nursing him and changing him. I rocked him and bounced him, but nothing seemed to help.

After thirty minutes of not knowing what to do, I walked two doors down and woke up my mom. "Mom, can you help?" I felt so weak at that moment. I was supposed to be the mom, and I was going to my mom for help.

My mom came and bounced Cory, but he continued to cry. Thankfully, after an hour he settled down and went to sleep. The same thing happened over the next two nights, and on those nights I had to ask for help again. I'm happy to report that things got better after that, but I'll never forget those moments of being humbled by turning to my mom for help. It's never easy!

Asking for Help Is Never Easy

Maybe you're like me. I wanted to be a great mom, but I needed help during some moments, even though I didn't want to admit it.

I was the student who would read the chapter three times instead of asking the teacher for help. (Or I'd skip that question completely.) I didn't like asking for help when my car started making a funny noise. This turned out to be a *huge* problem when my brakes failed while I was driving with my baby in the car. I didn't like asking my mom for money for diapers when my money ran out. And I especially didn't like asking for advice when my baby seemed to be especially fussy or tired. The thing was, my pride not only hurt me, but it also hurt my child. When I wasn't able to help him as I should, he was the one who suffered.

Eventually I had to start asking for help, if not for me, then for my baby. Here were a few things we needed:

1. *I needed sleep.* If you've already had your baby, then you know how often he or she wakes up during the night. I went from sleeping in until 10:00 or 11:00 in the morning when I was pregnant to being up half of the night—or so it seemed. Thankfully, I lived with my parents, and my mom was sometimes available to watch Cory when I needed a nap. I also learned to nap when he napped. (And I'm still an expert napper!) Sleep is one thing that will greatly help you as a mom. The whole world seems to be against you and everything gets on your nerves when you're tired. When you're rested, life works better and you feel more hopeful. Sleep is important; make sure you get some!

2. *I needed babysitting.* I started taking classes at my local junior college when Cory was only three months old. My mom worked, so she couldn't watch him. Thankfully, I had a friend who could. My friend Rosa also had a little girl, and she watched Cory for a few hours each day. She charged me very little, and her generosity made it possible for me to start my college education.

3. *I needed advice.* Babies come with a lot of responsibility. Sometimes Cory cried for no reason. Or he had a rash that wouldn't go away. Or he had a fever that seemed way too high. My mom gave me advice, but women at church helped me, too. They'd often dealt with the same issues before and gave me tips and suggestions when I had no clue.

4. *I needed hope.* Being a young, single mom is scary. Some days I wasn't sure if I could pull it off. Thankfully, two things helped combat those worries: reading the Bible and prayer. These are a few of the verses that reminded me I wasn't alone. Not only were there people in my life who wanted to help me, but God was there too.

   "I can do all things through Christ, because he gives me strength" (Phil. 4:13 NCV).

   "But the Lord is true, who will give you strength and keep you safe from evil" (2 Thes. 3:3 BBE).

   "He tends his flock like a shepherd: He gathers the lambs in his arms and carries them close to his heart; he gently leads those that have young" (Isa. 40:11 NIV).

Reading verses like these reminded me that God could take care of me. More than that, he wanted to! I learned to pray about my worries and concerns. I didn't use fancy words. Instead, I just talked to him like I'd talk to a friend. Sort of like this:

- "God, I'm really worried, and I'm not sure I can handle this."
- "God, I'm exhausted. I need your help to be patient with this crying baby."
- "God … *help!*"

It's crazy how simple prayers like that made a difference. The more I prayed, the more I saw things change for the better.

Of course, getting help depended on one thing: I needed to *ask*. It sounds easy, but if you're like me (proud and independent), it's not. Because I was a young mom, I felt I needed to prove myself. I wanted to show others I could care for my baby. I wanted to show people I could go on to do good things with my life in my own strength.

But the truth is, I had nothing to prove. I *was* a good mom. And if you love and care for your child and are trying your best, you're a good mom, too!

I also realized that *every* mom needs help. Moms who are married and have jobs and all the money they need still need help too. They have people watch their babies so they can sleep. They hire a babysitter so they can work. They ask for advice. They need hope during those long sleepless nights. They turn to the Bible for guidance. They pray and seek God's help.

Don't feel like asking for help makes you any less of a mom. Instead, it proves you're a great mom because you're doing what you can to make things better for you and your child. God doesn't want us to feel alone or to think that we have to do everything ourselves. Admitting we need help is difficult, but finding a good support system is a great example to set for your child.

When You Don't Feel That Help Will Be There

I know that it's easy for me to talk about asking for help, but maybe you feel that help won't be there, even if you ask.

I remember when I first found out that I was pregnant. The hardest thing I had to face was telling my parents. Thankfully, my mom and stepdad handled it pretty well. There was sadness, worry, and even anger, but their reactions weren't as bad as other girls' parents. I've heard of some girls getting kicked out of the house, and of screams and rants. Some girls never have a good relationship with their parents after that.

Most parents calm down, but their hurtful words remain. It's hard enough to deal with a teen pregnancy, but trying to deal with parents as well can be an added burden.

Sometimes it's easy to forget that parents are human. Through your growing-up years, they mess up and hope you don't see. But when they blow it big and react out of anger and frustration, sometimes their emotions are a huge wall between you and them.

Can You Help?

It's natural during this time to feel regret; you wish you hadn't disappointed them. It's also natural to feel hurt. Even though you find yourself pregnant, every young woman wants her parents' love to be unconditional. And while you may want to hold a grudge, sometimes the best thing you can do to bring healing to your relationship is to take the first step. Taking the first step to reconcile a splintered relationship can be so hard, but this is an important life skill that will help you to build healthy relationships and keep them.

Here are three perfect gifts you can offer:

1. *Understanding.* Tell your parents that you understand their reaction. Tell them you probably would react the same way if it were your kid who was having a baby. Remind your parent that nobody is perfect … not even close.

2. *Grace.* Wait until the difficult moment passes, and later offer a hug to break the tension. Tell your parent that it must be hard having his/her role.

3. *Respect.* Ask your parents for advice on how to best care for this child. Your parents react BIG because they know your future will never be the same. Ask for advice on parenting or adoption and let your parents know that you don't want to have to face this journey alone.

Your parents will get emotional during other times in your pregnancy, guaranteed. It won't be easy for them to see you have to make adult decisions when you still have so much growing up to do, but when you are tempted to see your parents as the enemy, remember that the journey you face will be easier with them by your side.

If you don't think you can get help from your parents, maybe your willingness to offer grace and forgiveness will change things. Then again, there is a chance that it won't. There are some parents who still haven't grown up (even after becoming grandparents). There are some who face addictions and have emotional problems. There are some who will try to depend on you, who will want you to be the responsible one.

Many of the teen moms I've worked with find themselves in the situation of needing to be the grown-up. The best thing to do is to be respectful but also to set boundaries. You don't have to lend your parents money if you need it for diapers. You don't need to cover for your mom if she's cheating on your stepdad. You don't have to allow your dad to curse or say foul things around your child. If your parent is not willing to grow up, then realize that you have to do what's best for your child. Also, look for help from other caring people. You will still need help, but sometimes you'll have to look beyond your family to find it. Understand that there are other young moms who are facing the same things, and sometimes the best thing you can do is help each other.

Give and Take

If you're getting help from your parents, it's also good to be helpful to them. Don't expect your parents to completely change their lifestyle to fit your needs. And don't expect your mom (or dad) to be your only babysitter.

Also, consider:

- *Your parents aren't as young as you are.* Their energy levels cannot handle a new baby as well as yours can.
- *Appreciation goes a long way.* Thank your parents for the help they provide. Give small gestures of care back to them, such as a thank-you note, a batch of cookies, or an offer to make dinner.
- *Don't expect to get it all for free.* If you're living at home, try to contribute something to the household expenses, even something small. And help with the housework as much as possible. This will show your parents you do care and you are taking your responsibility seriously.
- *Work out a contract with your parents.* Know what help they are able to provide and what's expected of you in return. Clear communication stops arguments before they start.

A Young Mom's Needs

What do you need most?

- More time to study
- Help around the house
- My boyfriend to live up to his responsibilities
- A better job
- Organization
- My diploma
- Money
- Another me
- Help!

- *Know that change will come.* If you are still at home, do not expect to depend on your parents' good graces forever. Develop both short- and long-term goals for your future. Share these goals with your mom and dad and ask for their insight.

What are some other ways you can practice give and take?

My Life

I need fun time with my little girl, communication with my husband, friends. Oh, and a bigger paycheck would help!

— Travis, *Michigan*

I need time to myself! My husband just doesn't get it. He's away at work and at play, all the time. My time away is a half-hour at the gym. That's it ... except the dentist.

— Amanda, *Ontario, Canada*

Most people I know do not have children and always invite me to places where kids just don't mix. Have you ever tried to find a babysitter on a Saturday night with only two hours' notice? It's like finding a must-have Christmas gift on Christmas Eve.

— Desiree, *Texas*

There Was Another Teen Mom Who Needed Help

Mary, the mother of Jesus, is one of the most well-known women of all time. She was also a teen mom facing an unplanned pregnancy. Mary's story is one of my favorites!

What we know from reading the Bible is that Mary was just a young teenager when God sent an angel to send her a special message. What was that message? That she was chosen to have a baby boy, a son. God's son!

Mary was confused. She was a virgin. Yes, she was engaged to a man named Joseph, but things were different back them. Sex was saved for the wedding night, and so having a baby at this point was impossible for this young woman. (And how does having God's baby work?!) Thankfully, the angel told her, "The Holy Spirit will come upon you." Whew.

Still, Mary trusted God. She praised him, and she thanked him for trusting her with this responsibility. Out of all the women who ever lived, God chose a young, lower-class, teen mom to carry his son and raise him to adulthood.

Yet even though Mary went along with God's plan, she no doubt got a lot of criticism. "You're pregnant with God's baby? Yeah, right."

Even her fiance, Joseph, didn't believe her story. He was set to break off their engagement until he got a visit from an angel too. The angel came to Joseph in a dream. Talk about a wake-up call.

Can you imagine what Mary's family and friends said? Yet God did not leave her to face it alone. In fact, God brought Mary help through a very special person named Elizabeth, Mary's older cousin. Elizabeth also faced a surprise pregnancy. The angel mentioned this when he first visited Mary. It's as if the angel was reassuring her: "I know this is a shock, but I have someone to walk the journey with you."

You may notice a few things about this story.

1. Mary was signed up for a big task she wasn't prepared for.
2. Mary no doubt faced criticism from people around her.

3. Mary found someone to turn to—a friend who could help her succeed in her new role.

Elizabeth played an important part in Mary's life. We know this because the book of Luke begins by telling us Elizabeth's story first. Elizabeth was the wife of a priest. She was very old and had no children, but God blessed her in her old age by allowing her to get pregnant. After Elizabeth's story comes Mary's story, another surprise pregnancy. Can you imagine what a shock that was to everyone who knew both women? (Yes, I'm sure you can!)

Again, the cool thing is that the angel Gabriel told Mary about Elizabeth's surprise pregnancy. It's as if he were saying, "Look, there's someone in your same situation. Turn to her. She can help you."

Mary did go to Elizabeth. In fact, she lived with her older cousin for three months. Elizabeth was the first one who rejoiced over the child Mary held within her womb, and I imagine Elizabeth was there to encourage Mary as she coped with the idea of becoming a teen mom.

Like Mary, each of us should have people in our lives we can turn to for help, support, and encouragement. Being a mom isn't an easy thing, and facing an unplanned pregnancy is even tougher.

When I had my son at seventeen, there was a group of women from my grandma's church that supported me. They were the first ones who showed me that the child who was growing inside me was a gift. They gave me a baby shower, and they fought over holding my son after he was born. They helped in dozens of little ways.

As my son grew, there were other women I looked to for help. When I had two kids, I met a friend named Cindy. She and I were the same age, and we quickly became friends. Cindy and I supported each other by trading babysitting, talking about parenting problems, and encouraging each other. She was someone who was walking the same road, and her advice helped more times than I can count.

No matter who we are or where we live, each of us can look around and see the people we have in our lives. Some may cheer us on, some may guide our parenting, and others may just be there to walk alongside us. If the mother of Jesus needed someone to look to for support, shouldn't we? Everyone needs someone to provide a little help and support.

My Life

Asking for help makes me feel weak. Yes, I have a hard time admitting I can't do it all. I don't want people to think I can't do it. Instead I want them to say, "Wow, what a good mom." I'm always worrying about what other people think of me as a parent ... it's not a good thing.

— Diana, *Washington*

Asking for Help

Do you have trouble asking for help? Here are a few words of advice:

1. *Ask trustworthy people.* There are some people who can't even help themselves; don't trust them to help you.
2. *Swallow your pride.* It's okay to confess the fact that you need other people. It's okay to admit you can't do everything alone.
3. *Don't feel you always have to return the favor.* While we may say we don't want to bother anyone, in truth, we don't want to owe anyone. We feel uncomfortable about repaying another person's kindness. We don't like the feeling of outstanding debt. It's hard to ask for help. Really hard. But don't always feel as if you have to pay someone back. Accept help as a gift and know there will be a time when you'll be able to offer that gift to someone else.

When it comes to asking for help, we also sometimes "save up" for help in case we really need it. We think, *I may need help more next week, so I'd better wait until I'm more desperate.* Meanwhile, we're pulling our hair out.

Of course, there are some people who aren't fooled by our inability to do it all: our children. We may be able to keep up our appearance to the outside world, but the little ones with us day and night see what we're like under pressure.

"A volcano, in essence, is a natural thing that explodes under pressure," says Julie Ann Barnhill, author of *She's Gonna Blow*. "And that's exactly what can happen to us…. In an instant we can change from the peaceful, nourishing women we want to be into Mount Momma—spitting fire and brimstone at all who cross our path."[1]

Trying to please everyone all the time doesn't work. We turn our lives and ourselves into a frantic mess. In the end, our peace of mind and our children suffer.

"There's no use trying to paste on a happy face or a good attitude to show in public if our hearts are cluttered with hidden issues," says Elisa Morgan. "What's stuffed down in our hearts will sooner or later spill over into our days with our children, our neighbors, our coworkers, and God."[2]

If you need help, ask. Your children will thank you for it!

Guy Help

Authentic men aren't afraid to show affection, release their feelings, hug their children, cry when they're sad, admit it when they're wrong, and ask for help when they need it.

—Charles Swindoll, *author*

When it comes to asking for help with the kids, the first person young moms should naturally turn to is a husband or the father of their child. After all, you're on this journey together.

As one young mom commented, "I think mums and dads share the same role in parenting because they are both parents and they have a child together."

Some moms find great support from the man in their life. They are part of a relationship in which both partners work to love and support each other.

If you have a man in your life who has made a commitment to you and your child, there are things you can do to grow a relationship in which both partners' needs are being met. Relationships take a lot of work, a lot of time, and a lot of dedication. But when you work to build a special bond, all will benefit—you, him, and your baby. Here are some things you can do.

1. *Offer support and respect.* To get support and respect, you also need to give support and respect. Think about your actions and words. Do they build up or tear down your partner? It's easy to be quick with the tongue and dish out criticism. It's harder to praise what we appreciate. It's easy to think of ourselves first. It's harder to think about the feelings and needs of others.

2. *Strengthen your relationship as a couple.* Relationships are challenging to any loving and committed couple. They are even more difficult between young people who face the numerous challenges of school, work, friends, raising a family, and the added task of growing up themselves. To make a relationship work, you need dedication and time spent together. You need to share your dreams, your feelings, and have a willingness to work toward a shared future. You need to be able to communicate your needs and be willing to meet the needs of the other person. (Don't expect your partner to be able to read your mind!) Also, as Romans 13:8 says, "Don't run up debts, except for the huge debt of love you owe each other" (MSG).

3. *Share the parenting load.* Sharing parenting responsibilities is tough, especially if the parents live in different households. One thing to do is develop a parenting plan. Sit down together and discuss roles and responsibilities. Discuss issues concerning your child's health, safety, and development. Decide who will do what when it comes to raising your child. Also talk about what you can do to support the other person's efforts.

It may take time and energy to build a caring relationship, but your child will be the one who benefits the most. If your baby daddy is willing to try to be involved, give him grace and strive to do your part to work together.

My Life

Right now my boyfriend and I are going through a rough time. He can sometimes be selfish and stubborn. He still wants to do what he wants, even if it's not the best for "the family." I just think that this whole thing about being a father hasn't hit him.

— Katherine, *Texas*

Me and my boyfriend are creating a relationship not just for us but for our son. We both understand that this is our child. We are both going to be in his life. Even if we hate each other sometimes, we make sure we don't argue or fight around him.

— Diana, *Washington*

Lack of Guy Help

Experience is a hard teacher: She gives the test first, the lessons afterward.

— Anonymous

While many young dads freely give their care and support, there are even more baby daddies who don't. Fatherhood is not a high school elective. Many young dads have no idea what being a parent is all about. Some baby daddies may grow up and want to take on the role later, but some may never come around, and it's their loss. Know that you cannot change another person. You cannot make someone care. You cannot make someone responsible. The only person you can control is yourself. It's better to step away and give someone space to change and grow than it is to hang around and bring heartache and disappointment to you and your child over and over again. It's better to face life as a single parent with peace than bring in strife by trying to force another person to change.

When it comes to single parenting, one common emotion young moms have to deal with is disappointment. When you raise your child without a father (whether by your choice or his), expect your feelings to fluctuate.

"Because the traditional American dream of husband, home, and family is so emphasized in our culture, you will be going through a normal grieving period over the loss of this dream," says Andrea Engber, author of *The Complete Single Mother*.[3] Expect yourself to get angry and to be upset. Allow yourself to grieve. Our culture does not grieve these types of losses well, but they need to be grieved. It's okay to feel sad and upset over the loss of a father for your child. It's okay to grieve the loss of the dream of a family or what you imagined that family would one day look like.

Remember, just because your child doesn't have his father around doesn't mean that he won't have a wonderful childhood. He can, and you can find peace in being the mom you should be.

Cutting Out Guilt (It Doesn't Help!)

Okay, confession time. As a young mom I often didn't ask for help because of pride, but there was another reason too: guilt.

Young moms often feel that they did something wrong and it's their fault when there isn't a father involved. In some cases guilt is good. For example, earned guilt is another name for a conscience. It's okay to feel guilty if you run a red light or copy a term paper off the internet. This type of guilt is an inhibitor. This guilt makes you think twice before you get yourself into trouble. It works to help you make better choices.

Unearned guilt is unnecessary, and it shouldn't stop you from asking for help. Perhaps you feel guilty because you can't afford your own place, or you can't buy your baby the same things a two-income family can provide. If you're feeling unearned guilt, stop! Let it go. Many young moms feel guilty they can't give their child a father figure. The guilt provides nothing productive. It just makes you feel worse about yourself. You won't be able to overcome your guilt by

Handling Feelings about an Uninvolved Father

- Don't dwell on the idea that you are inadequate or that his rejection is because of a flaw in your character.
- Do think more about yourself right now and about your soon-to-be child. Your responsibility is to yourself, not to your child's father's emotional issues.
- Do ask yourself, Is it single mothering I am afraid of, or am I really upset over the father's reaction and possible departure?
- Don't try to counsel the father, help him cope, or apologize to him.
- Do accept responsibility for the decisions you are making now.
- Do acknowledge your feelings of regret or disappointment. Until you accept the reality of this loss, you are flirting with depression. [4]

doing everything yourself. Instead, you'll just be overwhelmed and exhausted!

My friend Amy recently told me, "Unearned guilt is often shame at the core. I've been told that guilt is about something we've done (earned) and shame is about who (we believe) we are. That has proven true for me. This distinction has allowed me to let go of shame many times and reject lies I was believing about myself. It's also helped me to make amends for earned guilt when appropriate, which helps me to let go and move on when I messed up or made a mistake."

If you feel shame, realize that it's often unfounded—it's nothing you've done. If you feel shame, pray for God to show you who you really are. He sees you as his special daughter, whom he loves very much!

My Life

Sometimes I get really sad when I think that my daughter's going to grow up not knowing her father. Most moms have a husband behind them for the extra support and late nights, and even though my family tries, it just isn't the same.

— Jessica, *Florida*

The biggest challenge in raising a child is doing it alone – trying to raise myself and my son at the same time. Also going to college, working part time, and so much more.

— Diana, *Washington*

Right now I'm doing my best to do both jobs as a mother and a father. I know there are some things I can't do, so I compensate and do the best I can.

— Jessica, *Florida*

And if you're feeling guilty, ask yourself whether it's true guilt or a lie. If it's true guilt, make changes or make amends and start doing things as you know you should. If it's unearned guilt, ask God to help you let it go. Unearned guilt can be axed when you realize you *are* trying to do the best for your child, and when you realize God can take your bad choices and turn them into good. Don't let guilt keep you from asking for help!

Supporting Cast

> *Some people can't believe in themselves until someone else believes in them first.*
>
> — From *Good Will Hunting*

In the movie industry, actors and actresses who support the main star are known as the supporting cast. They are the ones who pop in at the right time, give their dialogue flawlessly, and make the lead

Can You Help?

actor look good. While it's true that you are ultimately responsible for your child, don't fool yourself into thinking you can do it alone. Everyone needs a supporting cast.

Who do you have in your lineup? Maybe you have a special friend who doesn't care what your house looks like. Or a family member who thinks nothing of your old sweats and torn T-shirts. Perhaps you have a close companion who enjoys sharing leftovers with you and chatting about the day's events. Or maybe you have friends who enjoy hanging out and don't mind the noise of toddler tantrums.

Each of us needs someone we can turn to for advice, someone who can help us with child care or who can give us a ride to the store. Your supporting cast is key to your success as a parent. A supporting cast is built one person, one relationship, at a time.

Think about your lineup of friends and family members. In movies, the main star may have one person who acts as a quirky sidekick and another who is the "mentor" character, dishing out wise advice.

Now it's your turn. Sizing up your lineup will provide you with resources when you're looking for a little help. (Be sure to include their phone numbers for a reference!)

Who You Can Call When:

- You need child care:
- You need help with homework:
- You're afraid:
- Your child is sick:
- You have an accident:
- You want to exercise:
- You need help around the house:
- Your car breaks down:
- You don't have money for rent:
- You need legal advice:
- You just want to have fun:
- You are worried about your child:
- You want spiritual advice:

My Life

I get help from my mum or my fiance's mum because they have been through the parenting stages.

— Sarah, *Australia*

My husband, my friends, and my father support me. Having people to talk to, cry to, and lean on helps so much. My father has also saved us from being homeless or foodless a couple of times.

— Travis, *Michigan*

My mom helps me out sometimes, like the other day I was up with my son until 4:00 a.m. She took him in the morning so I could sleep. She also gives me lots of advice.

— Diana, *Washington*

Also, when you consider your supporting cast, think of it as a two-way street. Who can you support? Perhaps another young mom? Think about what you can do for her. Consider which of the above roles you can fill. When you practice reaching out, you will grow more comfortable with give-and-take. You can ask for help because you've offered help. You will learn the joy of supporting each other.

Emotional Help

> Timon: *Gee, he looks blue.*
> Pumbaa: *I'd say brownish gold.*
> Timon: *No, I mean he's depressed.*
> Pumbaa: *Oh.*
>
> — From *The Lion King*

Some days everything is great. You get a good grade on a test, your house looks halfway decent, and your child says please.

Then there are those days when life falls apart. The demands on your time, the money challenges, and a baby who needs you 24/7 make you feel like a deflated balloon. You're depleted. Wiped out. When you feel this way, here are some things to consider:

- *Let-downs are normal.* You are young, and you are facing a tremendous amount of responsibility.
- *It's okay to cry.* Tears have healing properties. Each of us needs a good cry every once in a while.
- *Give yourself a break.* Forget cleaning up the toys. Instead, sit outside and enjoy the sunset.
- *Seek support*, especially if you can't shake your depression. There are many people willing to listen, support you, and give you the help you need.
- *Be aware of your feelings* toward your baby's father, especially if there are unresolved issues between you.

Seeking help with your emotions is just as important as seeking help in other areas. Don't be afraid to reach out! Out of all a young mom's needs, emotional needs are most likely to be ignored. After all, you must eat to live, and you must work to support yourself. But it's much easier to push your emotions deep inside, telling yourself you'll deal with them another day. You may run this way for a while, but you won't run well. And soon you will break down altogether.

"Just as your car runs more smoothly and requires less energy to go faster and farther when the wheels are in perfect alignment," says Brian Tracy, author and speaker, "you perform better when your thoughts, feelings, emotions, goals, and values are in balance."

If this is something you need to work on, don't wait to start. If you find yourself stressed or grumpy:

- *Pause to ask yourself what's causing the problem.* Do you need more sleep? Someone to talk to? Time away? Help?
- *Figure out how to have this need met.* Even if you have to wait until the weekend to get a babysitter, looking forward to a break will lift your spirits.

- *Pray.* When I have a bad attitude, I find strength in turning to God. Sometimes the situation changes, but sometimes it's my heart that has the transformation. I can't explain what happens inside, but I've felt a difference time and time again after I pray.

God Can Help

Even if you have a great husband, a helpful family, and supportive friends, there will always be times when you need a little more help. People—as great as they are—cannot give you all the help you need. Only God can do that.

And God's not only willing to help; he wants to! The Bible says, "God gives a hand to those down on their luck, gives a fresh start to those ready to quit.... God's there, listening for all who pray, for all who pray and mean it" (Ps. 145:14, 18 MSG).

Personally, I've received help from God when no one else could help me.

- He's given me hope when I've been disappointed.
- He's given me courage when I didn't think I could go on.
- He's given me patience when all I've wanted to do is scream.
- He's even provided for my needs (physical, emotional, financial) when my eyes could see no way.

If you're wondering how you can get this type of help, all you have to do is ask. God doesn't need fancy prayers. He just wants you to talk to him. Why don't you try asking for help from the ultimate Helper? You won't be disappointed!

God wants you to turn to him. He loves to help. And he will answer your prayers in ways you never expect!

My Life

I find myself frustrated and especially worn out when I get back from school and work. I try to pay lots of attention to my son, but he gets really crabby at that time of day. I know he is probably tired from daycare, but it's so hard. It drives me nuts.

— Diana, *Washington*

I can lift my head as a young mom because I know the closer I get to God, the better the mom he makes me. I don't think I would even be married today if it weren't for God. He has been my strength.

— Laticia, *Oklahoma*

A True Friend Is Like This ...

The Broken Doll

What type of help do you need? Sometimes the best way to learn to receive help is to give it.

> One day my young daughter was late coming home from school. I was both annoyed and worried. When she came through the door, I demanded in my upset tone that she explain why she was late.
>
> She said, "Mommy, I was walking home with Julie, and halfway home, Julie dropped her doll, and it broke into lots of little pieces."
>
> "Oh, honey," I replied, "you were late because you helped Julie pick up the pieces of her doll to put them back together?"
>
> In her young and innocent voice, my daughter said, "No, Mommy. I didn't know how to fix the doll. I just stayed to help Julie cry."[5]

Think of three things you can do for a special friend today. Maybe she needs physical help, such as child care, a meal, or someone to wash the dishes. Or perhaps a shared moment of laughter, venting, or tears would help the most. Give her a call to find out. If she says she doesn't think she needs help, set up a time to get together. You may discover needs that she doesn't realize she has.

Parent Power!

How to Be a Good Parent from a Child's Point of View

1. I feel secure when adults run the household. Be the parent!
2. I feel loved when you care enough to set boundaries. Make and keep rules.
3. I get confused when you are unpredictable. Stay dependable.
4. I'm being me. Accept my immaturity.
5. I'm learning about myself. Teach me to understand my many feelings.
6. I depend on you to teach me correct ways to act. Catch me being good and tell me.
7. I can get embarrassed. Correct me in private.
8. I learn when I experience the results of my behavior.
9. Discipline with consequences.
10. I'm full of questions. Tell me answers or I'll get them elsewhere.
11. I need to feel included in the family. Assign household chores.
12. I learn to trust from you. Keep your promises.
13. I need to accept my mistakes. Admit you aren't perfect.
14. I copy your ways of caring for myself. Live a healthy lifestyle.

— Brenda Nixon, *Parent Power*[6]

What other things can you add? How can you be a good parent according to your child?

Live and Learn

Seeking help enables me to be a capable mother.

7

Can I Get a Break?

Recreation

What is this life if, full of care, we have no time to stand and stare?

— William H. Davies, *poet and writer*

I almost said no when a friend called me up. She wanted me to go to a football game with her, and a thousand excuses ran through my mind. First, I didn't know if my baby would behave. Was it too cold outside? Would the roar of the crowd scare him?

Second, I had things to do, like homework and laundry. I had a term paper due on Monday, and if I didn't get laundry done over the weekend, I'd be in big trouble during the week. I still didn't fit into my "before pregnancy" clothes, and I didn't have that many clothes that fit.

Yet something inside told me that I needed to get out. I'd gone from having fun every weekend with friends to not getting out at all. It was okay to have a little fun, wasn't it?

I ended up going, and it was indeed fun. It was nice to be surrounded by people who were having fun watching the football game. It felt nice to breathe the fresh air. It felt wonderful to spend time with a friend.

In fact, did you know that God created a natural break for us when he created the world? In the first book of the Bible, Genesis, we learn that God created the world in six days. During those days he

Murphy's Laws of Parenting

- The later you stay up, the earlier your child will wake up.
- For a child to become clean, something else must become dirty.
- Toys multiply to fill any space available.
- The longer it takes to make a meal, the less your child will like it.[1]

And guess who's doing the staying up, cleaning up, and cooking—you! If you're worn out as a mom, you're not alone. All moms feel exhausted and overwhelmed at times. The reasons are clear:

- Lack of sleep
- Too much fast food
- Little exercise
- Frazzled nerves
- Demands that make you try harder to perform better
- No time for fun

The needs of our children and our lifestyles are endless. Where did all our free time go? Not too long ago you may have been a get-out-and-party girl. Now your idea of fun is squeezing in a few minutes on the phone or vegging in front of the TV. Who has time for recreation?

made the sky and the land, the air and the water, the plants and the animals—all the animals, including the fish and the land creatures. He also created man.

Then, on the seventh day, God rested. Did he need to rest? No. God is over everything. He never gets tired, and he never needs a nap. Instead, he chose to rest on the seventh day to be an example for us. We need to do the same. Many families consider Sunday their day of rest. It is often a day of putting aside work and being together. For many people, that also involves going to church. But however you spend your restful Sunday (or Sabbath), know that God designed things that way. He knows that people can go only so far before crashing. So, see, having a break isn't a selfish thing. In fact, it's by design.

24/7

The watchful mother tarries nigh, though sleep has closed her infant's eyes.

—John Keble, *British clergyman and poet*

I have to admit that I'm not always a fun mom. I'm better about washing dishes or doing homework than just playing, but I'm learning to do better. Just as we need to take time to have fun as a mom, we need to take time to have fun with our kids. This can happen when we remember what it was like to be a kid.

What do you remember most about being a kid? What were your favorite memories? Just because you're a teen mom doesn't mean life always has to be filled with conflict and struggle. You are the only mom your child has, and it's up to you to make great memories.

How do you do that? To get an idea of what things will mean the most to your children, think about some of your own favorite memories.

1. What was your favorite pastime as a child?
2. What was something fun you did with a sibling as a child?
3. What was your favorite meal?
4. What were some of the most memorable books you read?
5. Think of one particularly memorable event.
6. What scent or sound immediately takes you back to childhood?
7. What meaningful advice did you receive from an adult?
8. Think about someone who influenced your life profoundly.
9. Think about your proudest moment.
10. What made you laugh the most?

Make a Memory

Make a memory with your children,
Spend some time to show you care;
Toys and trinkets can't replace those
Precious moments that you share.
Money doesn't buy real pleasure,
It doesn't matter where you live;
Children need your own attention,
Something only you can give.
Childhood's days pass all too quickly,
Happy memories all too few;
Plan to do that special something,
Take the time to go or do.
Make a memory with your children,
Take the time in busy days;
Have some fun while they are growing,
Show your love in gentle ways.

— Elaine Hardt, *poet*[2]

Next, make a list of fun things you can do with your child. They can be things you can do this year or next year or five years from now. It doesn't matter when. What matters is that you take time to make memories.

You will have fun too. When you laugh with your children, you get the benefit of laughter. When you snuggle up to watch a movie, you get to relax. When you play at the park, you get the benefit of fresh air and exercise. You are reminded that life can be fun, and you teach your child the same.

My Life

Mothering isn't the hard part. It is all my other responsibilities that drag me down—work, school, household chores, and extended family.

— Jessica H., *Montana*

Free time is spent picking up, zoning out, or catching up on sleep.

— Travis, *Michigan*

Sometimes I get really stressed about being a single mom. There is never anyone to take over in the middle of the night, or anyone to change half the diapers, or just to take over when you need a nap.

— Jessica, *Florida*

Moms Need a Break

If you talk to any young mom, she'd agree that taking breaks is important, but getting away is the hard part. Sometimes it's challenging due to a packed schedule. Other times it is just too much work—finding a baby-sitter, making plans, and justifying money spent for fun. It doesn't help matters when you attempt to go out in the evening and your child doesn't want you to go. It's hard to walk away from those tears.

A doctor's appointment must be kept. A trip to town for diapers is a no-brainer. Yet time planned for fun isn't crucial—or is it?

- *Having fun makes for fun.* As moms, we think that devoting all our time to family responsibilities is part of the job description. Yet how does it make you feel when you follow the same old routine without a break? Listless, tired, bored. A mom who takes time to have fun is a fun mommy to be around.

- *Balance is better.* The ancient Greeks had a saying: Nothing overmuch. This phrase speaks to the necessity of balance. Balance is important in work, play, exercise, and even in quietness. It's good to work hard, but be sure to balance work with things that bring you joy.
- *Interests make all areas of life interesting.* "The effect of having other interests beyond those domestic works well," said Amelia Earhart, pioneering pilot from the 1930s. "The more one does and sees and feels, the more one is able to do, and the more genuine may be one's appreciation of fundamental things like home, and love, and understanding companionship."

My Life

I turn on my music whenever I start feeling worn out or am having a hard time with my son. I also drink lots of black tea to keep myself going, and take my son outside as often as possible. (He's much happier outside.) It also refreshes me!

— Simone, *New Zealand*

You need a break from your child, but if that isn't always possible, take a break with your child.

When was the last time you really played with your child? I mean the get-on-the-floor, roll-around-and-act-like-a-puppy type of play? Not too recently? Me neither.

It's hard to take time to play when there are so many other things to do. We feel guilty. But guilt shouldn't be a factor. Instead of considering yourself lazy when you take time to play, consider yourself smart. A smart mom knows that the clean laundry won't be remembered as much as the silly-face game. "It's up to us to seek out the little pieces of life that will become our children's memories," says author Sylvia Harney.[3]

Mom, You Need a Time-out

The dictionary definitions may not have changed since you've had your child, but perhaps your own definitions have.

Time-out: Once thought of as punishment. Now considered a much-desired, much-deserved break.

Quiet: Once avoided at all cost. (After all, what kind of fun can you have without noise?) Now treasured, sought after, and longed for.

Not only is playing fun, it's important for your child's development. Children learn about the world as they squeeze squeaky toys, crawl under tables, and peek out from behind their blankies. In fact, many developmental experts claim play is the "work" of children.

"A three-year-old child is a being who gets almost as much fun out of a $56 set of swings as he does from finding a small green worm," said journalist Bill Vaughan. Isn't that the truth! How many times has your child ignored the toy while playing with the box it came in? A son of one of my friends loved to play with a bathroom plunger. It was his favorite toy! (Don't worry: she bought a new one just for him.)

But older children shouldn't have all the fun. Babies love songs and fun interaction. You may be surprised how fun and refreshing playtime can be for you too. Here are some fun songs to sing and play. If you can't remember the words, ask another mom to help.

- "Peek-a-Boo"
- "Pat-a-Cake"
- "Head-Shoulders-Knees-and-Toes"
- "This Little Piggy"
- "Itsy-Bitsy Spider"

Copy Cat

Not wasting a moment, a child leaps from sleep and skips into a wonder-filled day.

"Ah!" says the wise mother, "An example to follow."[4]

Family time isn't only about playtime. There are quieter, gentler moments that mean just as much.

"As mothers, none of us want to look back in regret that we did not take our children to the playground, kiss them, hold them, and put them to bed," says Heather Hurd, author of *A Book of Hope for Mothers*. "The time we spend with our children when they are young is irreplaceable—for them and for us."[5]

One of my favorite things when my son was a toddler was to lay down with him before nap time. We would sing his favorite songs until his eyelids fluttered and he drifted off to sleep. Sometimes I would stop singing and just listen to his small, squeaky voice. The best part was when he'd forget some words and make up his own, singing with gusto all the same. It was times like this when my son and I learned to enjoy each other's company. And on the occasions when we both drifted to sleep, we just enjoyed being close and listening to each other breathe.

My Life

On the weekends I try to take my son somewhere special, like the beach, getting ice cream, or going for a ride on a train.

— Simone, *New Zealand*

My idea of fun used to be going out with my friends to the mall, movies, hanging out all night, and driving around town with the top down on the Jeep. Now fun is spending time with my baby girl.

— Nina, *Texas*

Laughter

Laughter is the sun that drives winter from the human face.

— Victor Hugo, *French poet, dramatist, and novelist*

What makes you laugh? TV sitcoms? Friends? Your child? YouTube videos? Whatever it is, you need more. "People who laugh actually live longer than those who don't laugh," says James Walsh, author of *Laughter and Health.* "Few persons realize that health actually varies according to the amount of laughter."

While comedy is good, one of the most important aspects of laughter is learning to laugh at yourself. Life doesn't have to be as serious as we make it. In fact, life is easier to deal with when we see the humor.

For example, one young mom found humor in a situation that could have upset her.

"One of the funniest things happened on the city bus," she said. "My son and I were out for the day and an older lady began asking about my son. She said, 'His mother must be very proud of him.' She thought I was baby-sitting! I had a good laugh about that later."[6]

Just like you plan what to cook and what to watch, consider planning at least one thing a day to make you laugh!

Why Laugh?

- *For the exercise.* Author Norman Cousins once said, "Hearty laughter is a good way to jog internally without having to go outdoors." Did you realize a hundred good laughs have been compared to ten minutes of rowing?
- *For the community.* Want to get to know someone better? "Laughter is the shortest distance between two people," says Victor Borge, Danish entertainer and pianist. When you laugh with someone a special, inexplicable bond is formed.
- *As a stress-reliever.* "Laughter is a powerful way to reduce tension and stress, creating a sense of well-being, increasing

contentment and alertness, helping us place the problems and difficulties of life in context," says Dr. Patrick Dixon, an English physician and author.

- *For good health.* "The two best physicians of them all are Dr. Laughter and Dr. Sleep," quips writer Gregory Dean Jr.

Take Time to Exercise! (Yes, It's Worth It)

There are some people who love exercise. For the rest of us, we do it because we know our muscles need to be strengthened, our heart needs to pump, and our pores need to sweat. "But why should I?" you ask. After all:

- You power-lift your twenty-pound baby from his crib, morning, nap, and night.
- You do "buns-of-steel" squats picking up toys off the floor and putting them into the toy box.
- You work your biceps and triceps scraping strained peas, carrots, and squash off the kitchen floor.
- You get a cardio workout running after your fifteen-month-old.

Yes, being a mom is a good workout, but we also need to make time for planned exercise, such as going for a walk or playing tennis with a friend.

The physical benefits are easy to see:

- Stronger heart
- Weight control
- More energy
- Increased strength
- Greater ability to fight illness
- Clearer thoughts

And there are also the spiritual and mental benefits.

"Like it or not—and I don't always like it!—good physical condition (or lack thereof!) does play a crucial part in our climb to sanity,"[7] says Julie Ann Barnhill, author of *She's Gonna Blow*. Our thoughts are more positive and our minds are clearer when we get our body moving and our heart pumping.

"I have a much more positive mood after I've gone for a walk," says one young mom. "It speeds up my metabolism, and I can think more clearly and feel more refreshed."[8]

You can also get your kids involved in exercising with you! Take them for walks, pushing a stroller. Dance in the living room together. Do an exercise video off of YouTube with your child by your side. Maybe create a star chart to keep track. Give yourself a star for doing something every day and then treat yourself to a fun day out when you finish a month.

For myself, when I take time to exercise, I usually start out grumpy, depressed, and overwhelmed, but as I move, the irritations seem to scatter. My problems may not be solved when I finish exercising, but I feel stronger and ready to tackle them.

My Life

My favorite recreation is jogging. Since I started, I have felt so much happier! I feel free from everything. It's twenty minutes when I don't have to worry.

— Amanda, *Ontario, Canada*

Young Fun

Live and work but do not forget to play, to have fun in life and really enjoy it.

— Eileen Caddy, *writer*

How would you define fun? I'm sure your definition has changed since becoming a mother. Sometimes it's as if you're pacing the sidelines with your baby while everyone your age tries on silly outfits at the mall, primps for the prom, or rides the rapids on their senior trip. Normal teen stuff seems far away.

But maybe your idea of fun has changed for the better. Many young moms I've talked to say having their babies took them out of destructive lifestyles.

"I was a pretty crazy person before I had my son; getting into trouble was fun for me," said one young mom. "Now fun is spending time with my family, going to the park, and watching my son learn and grow."[9]

There are others who try to mix both worlds—being a teen and a mom. "For fun I hang out with friends, go to dance clubs, bookstores, and take my daughter to the park for walks," said another young mom.[10]

Becoming a mom doesn't mean you have to give up everything fun about being young. It doesn't mean you have to wear sweats all day or go to bed at 9:00 p.m. But it does mean being responsible for the type of fun you choose.

It also may mean making choices that your friends don't understand. There will be times when you'll have to say no to inappropriate fun, like wild parties or all-night street dances.

For me, before I had my son, a good party or driving around in search of hot guys was my idea of fun. Afterward, it had no appeal. I didn't want to take my baby into that atmosphere. But not only that, as I grew up a little, those activities no longer sounded fun.

And boy, am I glad. When my son was a few years old, I ran into some of my old friends. By this time I was attending college and enjoying time with my son and new husband. But they were still doing the same old thing: searching for the perfect weekend party.

"When I first had my daughter—being a breast-feeding young mom—I couldn't just go 'out' with the girls anymore," said one young mom. "The sad part is most of them still don't get it!"[11]

Of course, there are still things you can do with your friends. Here are some ideas:

- After the baby's snuggled in her crib, you can have good friends over to watch a movie and munch on popcorn.

- Do each other's nails like you did when you were kids!
- Cook a gourmet dinner together.
- Go to the beach and play in the sand.
- Take a road trip and visit local attractions within an hour's drive.
- Plan a "just because" party, complete with a cake and party hats.
- Get together for a night of board games.
- Start a private reading group, and meet once a month to discuss the books.

My Life

For fun I blow off steam with my girlfriends. We talk, laugh, be silly. If our budget allows, we go out dancing. I write, rent movies, normal stuff. My idea of fun has changed. It's not just "Okay, I need twenty bucks to go out tonight, what am I wearing?" It's more like "Who's babysitting? Okay, she charges ten bucks. How far will I be if I'm needed? If my daughter wakes up at eight a.m., will I be able to deal with five hours' sleep? Are we going someplace safe?"

— Travis, *Michigan*

Me Time

Recreation isn't always about doing things, going places, and spending time with people. It may mean being alone. Whether or not being alone appeals to you usually depends on how you are wired. Are you an extrovert or an introvert?

Extrovert. An extrovert gets energized when she's around people. She's most comfortable in social settings, and being alone wears her out. She says what she feels (sometimes without thinking), and she isn't afraid to show her emotions. Recreation to an extrovert means doing something with someone else. It's getting out.

Introvert. Spending time alone and gathering her thoughts are what gives the introvert energy. She is more quiet and reserved, and she likes to keep her feelings private. Being around people may make her stressed or overwhelmed. She'd much prefer having a whole day alone to think, read, or do projects.

Of course, most of us are a mix of both. We enjoy being with others, but we also need time by ourselves. Sometimes your "me" time, can also include "he" or "she" time if you choose to spend it with a husband, boyfriend, or friend. What sounds like fun to you?

My Life

I get refreshed by talking to others. Getting everything that's bottled up out.

—Jessica, *Florida*

Sometimes I turn up my favorite music really loud and jump and dance around the living room. I also correspond with friends overseas, go to cafes, and go to plays. I daydream about my future — about getting married, about traveling the world, about the different types of work I wanna get into.

—Simone, *New Zealand*

My "me time" is when my daughter goes to bed. That's when I do housework, take a bath, and read. It's my time to get things done around the house and to pamper myself.

—Jamie, *Montana*

Feed Your Spirit

Just like our minds and bodies need time to get refreshed, our spirits need to be replenished as well. I know my day always goes better when I take time at the beginning to read my Bible, pray, and spend time with God.

In the Bible, Psalm 63:1 talks about an inner thirst for God. David, a king of Israel, wrote, "O God, you are my God, earnestly I seek you; my soul thirsts for you, my body longs for you, in a dry and weary land where there is no water" (NIV 1984).

If your inner spirit feels discontent—feels like it's missing something—time with God may be exactly what you need. Feeding your spirit doesn't have to be mystical and weird. And you don't have to wait to attend church on Sunday to give it a try. You can:

- Pause and say "thank you" when you see a lovely sunset.
- Pull out your Bible and read a few Scripture verses when your child is taking a nap.
- Write a letter to God, letting him know how you feel.
- Sing an old Sunday school song to your child.
- Talk with a friend, sharing the good things God has done in your life recently. And listen as she does the same.

My Life

There are times where I doubt myself, where I think that nobody cares, where I just don't know if I can keep going anymore—that's when I pray. I find that after I pray I feel like a huge burden has been lifted off my shoulders, and I feel this deep sense of peace.

— Simone, New Zealand

If you're ready for some recreation—whether it involves your mind, body, or spirit, check out these activities for fresh ideas!

Think outside the Box

New Ways for Having Fun

When you make plans with friends, your guy, or your child, do you do the same old things because it's what you've always done? Take a moment to think outside the box. Think about adventure and variety. Then fill in these blanks:

- Next time I got out to eat, one new food I'd like to try is:
- One fun activity I'd like to attempt is:
- Someone who seems fun to hang out with is:

Also, now that you're a mom, you should think about "wise fun." Here are some questions to ask yourself before going out:

- Is this a safe and secure environment?
- Do the people I'm with respect me? Are they caring and supportive?
- Is this an environment where sincere, trusting relationships can be built?

Finally, remember the delightful experiences you had as a child and try to recreate them.

- The things that made me laugh were:
- The things I liked doing with friends were:
- One thing I enjoyed and want to do with my child is:

Not Guilty, Your Honor

Ax the Guilt

Ever feel guilty for having time away? Read this poem.

Mother-guilt is attached to the umbilical cord, but it stays with you
    for life.
You feel guilty about what you do and guilty about what you don't do.
Guilty when you leave them and guilty when you pick them up.
Guilty about what they eat, what they don't eat, and even what they
    might eat.

Can I Get a Break?

The guilt gets you at night, on the train, standing in the school play-
ground, and especially when you've left them when you have a
break.
Then it usually gets attached to your purse and leads you to a toyshop.
What mothers need is a jury of twelve good and true mothers to stand
up and say, "Not guilty, your Honor."[12]

List five things you feel guilty about, then take time to consider this question:
Should these things make me feel guilty?

Take Time to Laugh

Humor Collection

Need a good laugh now and then? Create your own laughter by starting a
"Belly Laughs Collection."

- Watch YouTube videos or GIFs that make you laugh.
- Write down the funny things your child says or does.
- Keep a journal of humorous things that happen to you.
- Pick up costume pieces, such as glasses, noses, and funny hats. Keep
  them around for days you just want to goof off.

Take Time to Play

Just for Fun

Want something fun to do with your child? I love to color or draw picture or
bake cookies and decorate them. Search Pinterest boards for fun ideas of things
to do with your kids, using only the things in your house.
Here are some more ideas:

- Build a fort with pillows and couch cushions. Wad up newspaper to
  make balls. Then take turns tossing the balls into the fort, with someone
  inside to catch the balls.

- Build a dollhouse together using boxes. Ask your child to find small objects to use as furniture.
- Read a book aloud while the rest of the family listens and paints with watercolors.
- Let your child help you make play dough by mixing one part water, one part salt, and three parts flour. Then be sculptors.
- Make "ooze dough" by mixing two parts cornstarch and one part water. See what you can do with it. Swirl different colors of food coloring into it.
- Make hand shadows on the wall by darkening the room and shining a light on your hands.
- Play some of your child's favorite music and move to the music together.[13]

Live and Learn

A happy, relaxed mom makes a happy, relaxed home.

8

What's Most Important?

Perspective

Greatness is to take the common things of life and walk truly among them.

— Ralph Iron, *author*

Forty-three years ago a single young woman was about to give birth. She didn't know how she could afford a child without her parents' help. She hadn't talked to her former boyfriend in months. She had no idea how to reach him or how to tell him she was having his child.

This young woman attended church some, yet her dialogue with God was stilted. How could God let this happen to her? What would her life be like now? A baby girl was born, and upon holding her child, this young lady knew things would be okay. Perhaps this baby was a gift, not a burden as she supposed.

This woman raised her daughter the best she could, and while she wanted to give her child more than she had, history has a way of repeating itself. When the daughter became a young woman, she found herself in the same situation: living at home, pregnant, and scared.

The daughter knew she could raise this child. After all, her mom had done it. But what would her life be like? How could God let this happen to her? If you haven't guessed already, I was the daughter born to a single mom, and history repeated itself when I became a teen mom.

Now, if you take this story at face value, I am nothing more than a statistic. According to government research, most daughters of young mothers will be teen mothers themselves. They face lives of hardship, live on welfare for the most part, and become a burden rather than an asset to society.

Yet I am not a statistic. Why? Because God doesn't do statistics.

After I had my son, I tried to have a new perspective. I tried to think of what I could accomplish rather than what I couldn't accomplish. I saw myself as a positive influence on my son, and I tried to live up to that.

I had hope in my heart, and I started walking God's way. God brought an amazing Christian man into my life. John is a wonder-

Keep Things in Perspective

Teens make good and bad decisions every day. Lots of them. Most aren't as visible as teen pregnancy. Perhaps you think that's unfair. Your choice is leading you to make decisions you weren't prepared for.

You may not have been prepared to be a teen mom, but you can be a good one. By choosing to have your baby, you're already taking responsibility. You're choosing life for your child, and you're trying to do your best.

Today is the day you can make a good decision. Today is the day you can reach out to another mom. Today is the day you are loving your child. Trust that as you do more of all three, it'll be easier to do them more. You can focus on all three if you have the right perspective.

ful husband to me and a father to my son. John was drawn to me because of my positive outlook on life, despite my circumstances.

I'm thankful that my mother chose life for me. I'm thankful that when I questioned my future, God gave me hope.

History has a way of repeating itself in families, but God's history of setting things right trumps our history of messing up every time.

God has a history of seeing something no one else does. God's eyes see right through any outward characteristics or national statistics. His eyes scan down to the heart.

Have you ever felt like your decisions have ruined all your dreams? Trust that God's dream is to turn a mess-up into a miracle. He's a *big* God with *big* dreams—a God who sees the future, sees the past, and has a perfect plan for you and for me. That's the perspective we need to focus on.

Getting Perspective

You can learn many things from children. How much patience you have, for instance.

—Franklin P. Jones, *writer*

Ugh. Sometimes being a parent can be so frustrating. Just as you're finally working on your English essay or you're at a good place in the movie, your child needs your attention. It's as if he has an internal sensor that says, "Start crying, kid. Your mom is really busy now."

Of course, when is a good time to be interrupted? Something always fills our time or takes our attention. That's where perspective comes in. Perspective is viewing what happens today in light of the future. It's considering what's really important and contemplating what will matter to us five, ten, or twenty years from now. Then we can plan our time and our goals accordingly.

My Life

My fiancé and I were both excited about my pregnancy until reality set in. Then we were scared that we wouldn't have enough money, enough space in our apartment, and worried that I wouldn't be able to finish school. After we talked to some of our friends, we realized that we had plenty of support and would be able to figure things out.

— Amanda, Ontario, Canada

Change of Perspective

When we become mothers, we think about things we never considered before, such as being a good role model or scheduling play into our day. We worry about vaccinations, pollution, and too much sex on TV. We see the world in a different light, mainly because we've brought a precious child into it.

Here's another example of perspective:

Once there were two shoe salesmen who went to Africa to open new sales territories. Three days after they arrived, the first salesman faxed a message: "I will be returning on the next plane. I can't sell shoes here. Everyone goes barefoot all the time."

There was no report from the second salesman for about two weeks. Then came a fat, airmail envelope with this message for the home office. "Fifty orders enclosed. Prospects unlimited. Nobody here has shoes."[1]

When you became pregnant, it may have been difficult to consider your pregnancy in a positive light. You may have been like the first shoe salesman who simply focused on the negative and felt like walking away.

Of course, you couldn't walk away. You're a mom now. Now you see the world with a mother's eyes.

My Life

Before I was pregnant, all I wanted to do was get out of my mom's house. Now that I have a child, I wish I could just go back and have my mom take care of me — but that's not possible.

— Jessica, *Montana*

Being a mom has changed the way I think. I worry about things that I never worried about before. We went on vacation, and we had to fly. I have never had any problems with flying, but knowing that my baby was on the plane really upset me.

— Jessica, *Florida*

If I didn't have my daughter, I wouldn't be going to college or bettering myself. I would be one of those kids you see on the street drunk by noon. When I think of that, I appreciate her that much more.

— Jamie, *Montana*

You've discovered there is a second way to look at your situation. Like the second salesman, you see the potential. Motherhood has become a time to reconsider your future. A time to clarify your goals. Or maybe it's a time to take a different path.

Making Attitude Adjustments

One of the first things that may have changed when you became pregnant was your attitude. I remember the first few weeks I knew I was expecting. I was sick and miserable. I refused to go to school, refused to leave the house.

Gradually my attitude changed. Instead of feeling sorry for myself, I thought of the good to come out of it. I was going to have a baby, a beautiful baby.

"Our attitude will determine everything in our lives from whom we marry to what we do for a living," says Lucinda Basset, author of *Life without Limits*. "It will determine how we deal with our failures and how and if we achieve our successes; and it will determine our destinies."[2]

Stop and consider your attitude right now. How do you feel about where you are in life? How do you feel about your role as a mother?

Perspective means stopping to consider your various roles. It's weighing the importance of your relationships (as a wife, mom, friend, daughter) in comparison to the tasks you tackle every day. Take a minute and think of all the things you might do in one day.

1. Bathe and dress baby
2. Fix meals
3. Attend classes at school
4. Watch television
5. Check Facebook
6. Text or talk with friends
7. Visit your mom
8. Read to your child
9. Clean the kitchen
10. Invite a friend over for a meal
11. Surf the internet
12. Go to work
13. Shop at the mall
14. Call your grandma
15. Read your Bible and pray
16. Watch YouTube
17. Meet friends at the park
18. Do laundry
19. Go out drinking with friends
20. Play with your child on the floor
21. Spend quiet time talking with your husband or boyfriend
22. Complete a project at work
23. Write in your journal

What's Most Important?

Now ask yourself these questions:

1. Which tasks help you to contribute to what's most important?
2. Which ones do you wish you had more time for?
3. Other than taking time for fun and relaxation, which ones would you consider a waste of time?
4. How has your perspective changed after having your child?
5. Are there areas you need to look at with a new perspective?

A New Perspective on Guys

Young women, do you wonder if the guy of your dreams is out there? Do you think that even if you find him, he'll think you've made too many bad choices and he'll look away, walk away? Are you ready to be the one the guy of your dreams is looking for?

In God's Word we read, "Seek the Kingdom of God above all else, and live righteously, and he will give you everything you need" (Matt. 6:33 NLT).

As you wait for a good guy to give your heart and your life to, seek God. Give your heart to him, and he will help prepare it for your future husband.

I talk about how God brought me the man of my dreams as a single mom in my book, *Praying for Your Future Husband*. God has a good plan for you too! Remember that!

Don't give up. Trust that the right guy will come at the right time. Trust that God is already preparing his heart for yours.

Below is a song that my son Cory wrote as he waited for his future bride. Less than one year later he was engaged to her! Now, four years later, they're married with a two-year-old son and a baby daughter.

Right now, ask God to help you be "that girl" for a wonderful guy someday.

That Girl

That girl
I don't know her hair color
I don't know her smile
I don't know her laugh
I don't know the color of her eyes
Or her favorite song
I don't know her passions
I don't know the thing she hates
I don't know her face
I don't know where she likes to hide
Or the twinkle in her eye
I don't know if I know her
But I know she is that girl
I would give my life for that girl
I would give up everything for that girl

I would die for that girl
I would live for that girl
I would love that girl
I would care for that girl
I would take care of that girl
All for that girl

I know she is beautiful
I know she is smart
I know she is wonderful
I know she is funny
I know she is amazing
I know she is mine
I know she is that girl

What's Most Important?

She may not know it yet
For I surely don't
She may not love me yet
But I know she will
Because I know I will love her
With all that I have

She may not even know me yet
But she will know me more than anyone
She may have a past
Wrong things
Regrets
Sorrows
But I will not see these things
I will wipe away her sorrows
I will not remember her wrongdoings
I will not regret
Because if everything
She has ever done
Will lead her to me
Then I thank her past

So God I pray
I pray for that girl
I pray you let me wait
I pray you let her wait
I pray for her safety
I pray for her happiness
That Girl

— Cory Goyer, *April 2009*

How does it make you feel to know that there could be a guy out there thinking of you this way? Does it give you a new perspective? I hope so!

My Life

It helps to remember my child will be two only once. I don't know God's plans for the future, and I need to make the best of the time I have.

— Katherine, *Texas*

Mom, Others Believe in You Too

When I was a teen mom, I thought it was me against the world. I thought everyone would look down on me. I was sure that every time someone pulled me aside to talk to me, I'd hear words of condemnation.

Instead, I was amazed at how many people really cared about me. Time after time, men and women encouraged me, and I clung to their advice.

I asked my Facebook friends, "If you were having coffee with a young mom today, what encouragement would you give her?" Below is what they said. I hope you will be encouraged! I hope this will give you a new perspective. There are many people out there who *do* believe in you!

Your past in no way defines your future. Your path (if you take God's hand for the journey) is like the first gleam of dawn, growing ever brighter until the full light of day! (Prov. 4:18)

— Tanya

The way things seem now will not be that way forever. God's TRUTH is far different from the facts we see with our narrow scope of what we think of reality. The Israelites were standing at the edge of the sea with Pharaoh's army right behind them. Fact: They weren't gonna make it. Truth: God made a way!!!!

— Denise

What's Most Important?

Children of single parents can be found and used by God. God is the father to the fatherless.

—Pia

I was a teen mom at the age of 18. God can and will redeem the past into a wonderful future. God is the author of a good future. He will provide the way for it to happen. I never knew if we would make it as a couple being only 18 and 16 years old (my hubby), but here we are 30 years later and more in love than ever before. God is a good God.

—Angie

Being a mom so young forces you to grow up early. That is not a bad thing. Finishing school and caring for your child become your focus. I know a sweet girl who is now a successful school teacher. My grandson is 14. His dad and mom are great parents.

—Cindy

You can be a great mom at your age, as well! You will make mistakes, but seeking encouraging friends, looking for mentors, and educating yourself will make you a better mom than you thought you could be. I was a teen mom, and I messed up a lot of the times, but it goes by so fast and you will suddenly have teenagers yourself!

—Martha

Don't let anyone else influence your decisions. Too many people are absolutely certain they know what is best for another person. It's OK to listen to advice, but, in the end, only you know what is best for you and your child. P.S. I was not a teen mom, but I was single when I became a mom and there are still days now, ten years later, when I feel inadequate and immature. We are all human. What teen mothers need more than anything else is support, acceptance, and love!

—JC

Now, how about you? What advice would you give to another young mom? What encouragement could you give to change her perspective?

Future Thinking

Alice said, "Would you tell me, please, which way I ought to go from here?"

The Cheshire Cat responded, "That depends a good deal on where you want to get to."

Alice replied, "I don't much care where."

The Cheshire Cat responded, "Then, it does not matter which way you go. Any road will take you there!"

— From *Alice's Adventures in Wonderland* by Lewis Caroll

Where do you want to go from here? Just as the Cheshire Cat reminded Alice, you have to know where you're going if you want to get there.

Giving Up versus Looking Up

In working with young moms, I've seen two paths they usually choose. Some young moms feel that after having children their lives are out of control, so why bother? They've given up plans for college, and instead try to find any job to bring in money. They live where it's convenient, even if the neighborhood isn't very good. They hang out with anyone available, because any friend is better than no friend. They have a new relationship every month. Their perspective is short-range, and their future thinking doesn't go beyond what movie to watch next weekend.

There's a second group. They have a different perspective. Even though it takes more effort, these moms weigh their education options. They seek out appropriate day care and work at jobs with opportunity for promotion. These young moms think of future careers and trust that the time and energy they put into their goals will someday be rewarded. They either commit themselves to a relationship or date only guys who fit their requirements for a lifelong partner.

Of course, life isn't always so black and white. There's some gray mixed in there too. The first group sometimes makes great choices and things start to change. The second group doesn't get it right all the time, but at least they try. Sometimes they might even revert back to their old ways, but they don't stay there. Whenever they find themselves heading down the wrong path, they turn back to the direction that offers progress and a bright future. Whether we're in one group or the other, or somewhere in the middle, we all need help.

Which path are you taking?

Of course, just because we take time to plan our future goals doesn't mean we're in control of the future—no one is. Your baby gets an earache the day of your final. You discover a spit-up stain on your nicest skirt right before a job interview. Your car breaks down. Your company orders layoffs.

My Life

Getting pregnant was definitely a life-changing experience. I have become closer to God and overall a better person.

— Katherine, *Texas*

When I need some perspective, I turn to my grandma. In a time where woman's liberation is so dominant, I need a little old-fashioned advice. She reminds me of who God made me first: his child, a wife, and a mother.

— Laticia, *Oklahoma*

Looking at the "bigger picture" of parenting helps me to realize that my current situation will improve. It is just a matter of faith, time, and hard work. My son will get older, make friends, go to school, need me less. I will finish my studies, get a job, and have more time and money to pursue my dreams and goals.

— Simone, *New Zealand*

Future thinkers take these things in consideration and are willing to rework their goals. Future thinkers trust in God, the God who is in control. They pray about their decisions and understand that God sees the bigger picture. The well-known "Serenity Prayer," often attributed to theologian Reinhold Niebuhr, conveys this perspective well:

> *God, grant me the serenity to accept the things I cannot change,*
> *the courage to change the things I can,*
> *and the wisdom to know the difference.*

The Familiar Way versus the Right Way: Habits

If you could change one thing that you find yourself doing over and over again, what would it be? For me it's not paying attention when my children are talking to me. "Uh-huh," I answer automatically, without taking time to turn, make eye contact, and listen. This is a bad habit that I've gotten myself into—one that I'm working to change. Whenever I find myself doing it, I make an effort to pause what I'm doing, and to turn and look at my child right in her eyes.

I do have good habits too. One good habit I have is waking up early. (And to do this, I need to get to bed before midnight!)

Although it took planning to develop this habit (setting the alarm clock earlier each day), it's been worth the effort. I enjoy the quiet mornings when everyone else is asleep. It's then that I have time to pray, read my Bible, and contemplate my goals and dreams.

Then there are those habits I wish I'd break, like piling items at the bottom of the stairs because I don't want to make the effort to climb the stairs and put them away. This habit not only leads to clutter but also can cause someone to trip and fall.

But there are bigger issues than that. I have a habit of thinking of myself first. I have a habit of not addressing my child's disobedience as I should because at the time it's easier to let it slide. I have a habit of fibbing just a little when telling a good story, or not truly admitting how much I spent at the store. But these habits hurt me more than I think. They cause me to trip and fall daily. And as my children pick up the same bad habits, they will hurt them too.

They are all habits I'm working to break, and ones I can break with God's help. Like with anything else, overcoming bad habits takes work. I've overcome the habits of cussing a lot, of watching inappropriate movies, and of listening to music that doesn't have the best lyrics. I've overcome these habits with God's help, and I know he'll strengthen me as I turn to him when I have additional struggles. He won't give up on me, and whenever I ask for help, I feel stronger to stand up against what I don't want sticking around.

My Life

Parenting is scary. It has to be one of the hardest things to do. Deciding limitations, punishments, rules, expression of love and other emotions, there's so much to consider and decide on. No one's perfect, but any "good parent" tries to do their best.

— Katherine, *Texas*

Many Things Half-Done versus a Few Things Done Well

As moms we want to do it all: keep a perfect house, be a perfect student, love our friends and family in abundance. Of course, we can't do all these things perfectly.

The cartoon character Charlie Brown once said, "In the book of life, the answers aren't in the back." That's the truth! The answers to how and where you spend your time and energy are something you have to figure out. Here are some considerations to get you started:

- *Realize that time is limited.* We know this, but do we really live by it? In the Bible, King David says, "Teach us to number our days and recognize how few they are; help us to spend them as we should" (Ps. 90:12 TLB). This is awesome advice.
- *Realize that people matter most.* I've heard it said that you can tell which things people care about most by looking at their calendars and what they spend their money on. What do these two things say about you? Are you giving your time

and money to things, or to people? Things rust, break, and go out of style. Heart connections with people last a lifetime.

- *Realize it's better to do a few things well.* If you could do only a few things well, what would they be? If you spent ten years working on your fiction-writing skills, you might be able to have a novel published. You'd find the same type of success if you worked ten years as a painter or sculptor. And just think what type of parent you could be if you spent ten years working at being the best one possible!

This is not to say that you should give up housework, focusing only on your child. But when it comes down to either having a perfectly clean kitchen or spending a perfectly wonderful day with your toddler, only one matters most.

My Life

Sometimes it's hard to keep my focus. I have so many things going at once. So many things I need to get done. It can become overwhelming. It can be frustrating and confusing.

— Katherine, *Texas*

Priorities Mean Treasuring Every Moment

There have been many times when I've daydreamed about my children getting older. I try to imagine strolling through my home without tripping over a jumble of toys, or getting lost in a good book without being interrupted by children's shrieks.

Then the day came when I got a taste of what this would be like. My kids were spending the night with their grandparents. My house was quiet. The toys stayed in their toy box, but surprisingly, I didn't like it. When the next morning dawned, I was happy to have them back. I missed the smiles and laughter. I even missed the noise!

Sometimes when you're in the middle of a "parenting moment," it's hard to appreciate being a mom. My grandma is good at reminding me of how precious

Pearls of Wisdom

If you plant for days — plant flowers.
If you plant for years — plant trees.
If you plant for eternity — plant people.[3]

these moments are. "These are the best years of your life," she often tells me when I call. "Enjoy every moment." Okay, maybe it's not possible to enjoy every moment, but I'm doing a much better job of working at it!

My Life

As a young mom it's hard sometimes. I see other teens and the life they live. They are so carefree and irresponsible. For a millisecond I think, That could have been me. Then God gives me a reality check. Like having my four-year-old say, "You are the best mommy ever." Or my baby will touch my face and smile. Those things bring me back to what's important.

— Laticia, *Oklahoma*

What Are Your Priorities?

From the beginning, I knew that spending all the time I could with my son was important. But being young, I also knew that graduating from high school and attending college classes would benefit us both. I made it a priority to work on my education. It meant finding good child care and spending late nights doing homework after my son went to bed. But the benefits of my school years can't be denied. Education—both formal and informal—has transformed me into a mother my son can be proud of. And a woman I can be proud of.

Time Waits for No One

To realize the value of one year: ask a student who has failed a final exam.

To realize the value of one month: ask a mother who has given a birth to a premature baby.

To realize the value of one week: ask an editor of a weekly newspaper.

To realize the value of one hour: ask the lovers who are waiting to meet.

To realize the value of one minute: ask the person who has missed the train, bus, or plane.

To realize the value of one second: ask a person who has won a silver medal in the Olympics.

Time waits for no one. Treasure every moment you have!

— *Author Unknown*

Once I got married, my husband became a major priority too. From early in our marriage, I have taken time to show him he's important. I chat with him while he gets ready for work. I cook dinner most evenings, things he likes. I even watch sci-fi movies with him occasionally. We talk and laugh together and consider each other our best friends.

My kids are also a top priority. At a time in my life when outside activities such as book clubs or coffee time with friends interest me, I instead choose to spend time at home with my kids. When I'm able, I catch up with friends after my kids go to bed for the night.

Of course, I don't always know what's best at all times. I make choices, then I change my mind. I make commitments to stay close to home, and then I seek out friends because I feel lonely. One week I'll be on a healthy food kick, and I'll break out my low-fat cookbook and marvel my family with culinary creations. The next week, I'll get involved in a new project, and we're scarfing chicken fingers and mac and cheese.

Yet even when I change my mind and my daily priorities, I still keep things in perspective: God, husband, family, home, friends, work. I still try to consider how today's decisions affect my goals for the future.

Balance

In the end,
all of life,
all of mothering,
is all about balance.

Having balance means:

- Loving your child, yet taking care to discipline.
- Not focusing solely on your child, yet giving her the attention she needs.
- Providing friendship and accepting friendship in return.
- Looking for a heart-companion, yet becoming the person someone else can give his heart to.

Balance is:

- Planning for the future, yet trusting in a God who knows what's best.
- Working toward your education, but not getting too wrapped up in success.
- Telling someone what's on your heart and taking time to listen.
- Being a mom your child needs, yet stealing moments to contemplate your unique dreams.

If someone figured out how to balance all of life perfectly, her book would hit the *New York Times* best-seller list, and she'd be invited to every talk show. But seeking balance doesn't mean finding one place or one perfect schedule and sticking to it.

"Up-and-down rhythm can actually keep … life moving in a positive direction. Our lives are meant to be dynamic, not static," says Joanna Weaver, author of *Having a Mary Heart in a Martha World*. "Like a clock pendulum or the pump of an oil well, the rhythm actually generates energy for our lives. The truth is, we thrive on a life that is rhythmically balanced, not standing still."[4]

Yes, no. Work, play. Move forward, rest a while. Keeping life in perspective, keeping God and relationships in perspective. All of these will bring rhythmic balance to your life and your mothering. Check out these activities to help you do just that!

Please Don't Believe It!

What Pop Culture Tells Us

That size 12 is big.
That we must dress right, or end up in a "don't" column.
That we must constantly seek perfection.
The same information every month with different titles.
How to cook, eat, dress, behave, and think.[5]

Too many times we get our perspective from magazines that display airbrushed models on their covers, or from TV sitcoms where the scriptwriter, set director, and hair and makeup artists all work together to portray "reality." Personally, I get in trouble when:

- The latest catalogue makes me feel as if my clothes are out of fashion.
- The slim models make me feel frumpy and fat.
- The latest episode of HGTV makes my own place seem dingy and bland.
- Health magazines make me feel like a failure for not exercising often enough.

What's Most Important?

What about you?

- How do the models in the magazines you read affect your perspective about yourself?
- How do the articles in parenting magazines make you feel about your parenting abilities?
- How do romantic movies make you feel about being a wife or girl-friend? Or worse yet, how do they make you feel if you're single?
- How do songs on the radio make you feel about life? Excited? Hopeless? Do they make you think of life as a gift?

Next time you're reading a magazine, watching a movie, or listening to music, consider how you feel. Nix any media outlets that make you have a negative perspective on your life, your parenting, or yourself. Replace it with media that will encourage and inspire you. Then weigh how your perspective changes for the better.

From This Moment

It's What You Do Afterward That Counts

You may not have seen your pregnancy coming, or the changes that mothering would bring to your life, but what you did afterward is what counts. Take a moment and consider the things you did right:

- What did you do afterward concerning work or school?
- What did you do afterward concerning your friendships and other relationships?
- What did you do to help you become a good parent?
- What planning have you done toward a better future?

Now ask yourself what you can do from this moment on to improve in each of these areas.

Spreading the Love

An Example of True Love

An old man got on a bus one February 14 carrying a dozen red roses. He sat beside a young man. The young man looked at the roses and said, "Somebody's going to get a beautiful Valentine's Day gift."

"Yes," said the old man.

A few minutes went by and the old man noticed that his young companion was staring at the roses. "Do you have a girlfriend?" the old man asked.

"I do," said the young man. "I'm going to see her now. I'm taking her this." He held up a Valentine's Day card.

They rode along in silence for another ten minutes, and the old man rose to get off the bus. As he stepped out into the aisle, he suddenly placed the roses on the young man's lap and said, "I think my wife would want you to have these. I'll let her know that I gave them to you."

He left the bus quickly, and as the bus pulled away, the young man turned to see the old man enter the gates of a cemetery.

— Author Unknown[6]

None of us like the thought of losing the ones we love. How does this story put life and love into perspective for you?

If you could do anything for the person you love right now, what would it be? What's stopping you?

Habits Change Everything

Take a couple of minutes and consider your habits. Jot down your answers to these questions:

- What habits have helped you in life?
- What habits do you wish you could get rid of?
- What got you started on these bad habits?
- How did you train yourself for the good habits?
- How can you turn the bad habits into good ones?
- How do habits affect your parenting?
- Do you treat your child the way your parents treated you out of habit?
- How would you really like to treat them?

This, my friend, is perspective.

Live and Learn

Perspective helps me to focus on what matters most.

9

What Am I Here For?

Hope

You've heard bits and pieces of my story throughout the book, but this is the part I've been waiting to tell you. It's the part when Cinderella, who feels so abandoned and alone, discovers her Prince. It's more than this teen mom ever imagined, really. And it is the best part of the story for certain.

When I first met my baby daddy Rob (not his real name), I thought he was something special. He was a football player, an honors student, and very handsome too. The best part was that he liked me. I was head-over-heels excited. I thought I was in love.

"Dating" in my small town consisted of being together at dances, at sporting events, and in cars hidden away on dark country roads. Our relationship became physical even before we had a chance to get to know each other's heart. Then there were the attractions—mine to other guys and his to other girls—that caused all types of problems.

We dated from my sophomore year to my senior year, with more turbulence than a jet plane in a windstorm. When I found out I was pregnant, Rob was soon out of the picture.

My parents were upset, but they were committed to helping me stick it out. I'd already had an abortion the previous year—due to

Rob's insistence and my own fear—and I wasn't going to make that mistake again. Though he wanted me to have a second abortion, I couldn't do it. I already hated myself for the first one. I lived with the horror of the abortion decision every day and had nightmares about it every night.

You may remember that feeling of attending class, knowing the secret that you have a baby growing inside you. I felt hot and tense and unable to focus. Soon the word got out and rumors spread. Glances were cast my way as I walked down the halls. People whispered behind my back. My friends were awkward around me. Rob began dating someone else. I wanted to move away and never return. The next best thing was for me to drop out of regular school, which I did.

I was sick, tired, and getting bigger by the day. I enrolled in a school for needy teens and fit right in. This all happened during my senior year, and while everyone was attending Homecoming and Prom, I was staying up late watching old movies and sleeping until noon. What had become of my life?

I clearly remember waking up one day and flipping on my favorite soap opera, *The Young and the Restless*. What an appropriate title for what I was feeling.

I rolled onto my side, wrapped my arms around my expanding stomach, and considered what a mess I'd made of my life. What happened to my dreams, plans, and goals for a good future?

Then I remembered something. Like a ray from a lighthouse breaking through a foggy coastline, I thought of the stories I'd heard as a child while attending Sunday school. Stories of a God who loved me, not my performance. A God who accepted me as I was without needing to make myself look good.

So at that moment, I prayed. It wasn't elegant, but it was from the heart. "God, I've really screwed things up this time. If you can make things better, please do."

And then that beam of light touched not only my memory but also my heart. And in an inexplicable way, I felt different inside. Something birthed inside me. That something was hope.

And at that moment, my soul sang.

I couldn't count on people, but God proved I could count on him. I was unmarried, pregnant, angry, and lonely. God was okay with that.

> Hope is the thing with feathers
> That perches in the soul,
> And sings the tune without the words
> And never stops at all.
>
> — Emily Dickinson[1]

I didn't know where to go or what to do next, but the peace of God told me things would work out. I needed love, and he loved me. He wanted to prove I was someone special in his eyes—even when I felt far from special in my own.

Hope made its home in my heart that day. My life wasn't suddenly fixed. I still didn't know what to do with the mess I was in. I didn't have all the answers. But hope told me it would be okay. It was a miracle, and I was full of wonder.

My Life

When I place my hope in God, I am more positive, less stressed. I feel free.

— Katherine, *Texas*

Today can be a day you'll always remember. There is one day I remember well.

The day I gave my heart to God, I turned onto my side, wrapped my arms around my stomach, and prayed, "God, I have screwed up my life. If you can do better, please do." I remember that I'd turned off the TV because watching other peoples' problems wasn't helping mine. I remember I had a pink satin comforter. I remember the sunlight shining through the windows. And I remember the glimmer of hope that came when I prayed that simple prayer. Those memories will never leave me.

What are you going to do with today? Will today be a memorable one? Will this very moment be memorable? The choice is up to you.

This very moment you might be questioning your future. You may wonder whether you'll be able to finish school. You wonder whether your relationship will last. You're worried about the money you'll need for diapers. You question how you'll ever be able to handle being a mom while, in a way, you're still a kid yourself.

But someday you'll be looking back. What will you remember about today? Will you remember anything?

This day, like most days, can slip into nothingness. It could be long forgotten. There could be nothing special about it. Hanging out with friends, checking Facebook, watching a movie, eating the same type of food that you ate yesterday and the day before.

Or today could be a turning point. Today could be a day you will always remember.

- Today could be the day you look in your child's eyes or look at your expanding belly and make a promise to be a good mom and then take the first steps toward making that possible.
- Today could be the day you check into financial aid for college and fill out an application or sign up for classes to help you with your GED.
- Today could be the day you mend your relationship with your parents.
- Today could be the day you research more about your dream job.
- Today could be the day you end the relationship with the man who hurts you, cheats on you, and would rather party than be a good dad, and instead start praying for a godly future husband.
- Today could be the day that you surrender everything to God, the day you lay down your will for his.
- Today could be one you never forget.
- Today could be the day you turn to God, the day he changes your heart.
- Today could be the day that hope changes it all.

Hopeless Situations

Young Moms Need Hope

When sleep is a distant memory.

When your sweet little baby transforms into a monster-toddler.

When you have only ten dollars for the rest of the week.

When the only "men" who pay attention to you are your son . . . and your little brother.

When your best friend no longer calls.

When your schoolwork doesn't get done because you have to work late.

When life isn't what you signed up for.

When your "fat" clothes have replaced your "skinny" ones.

When you long for someone who understands.

When life seems hopeless.

— Tricia Goyer

What Hope Can Do

Have you ever felt hopeless? I can only guess the things that rob your optimism: guy problems, money issues, overwhelming responsibilities.

But those are only outside struggles. There are also inside struggles that can weigh you down. Sometimes you feel loneliness, heartache, anger, and despair. Other times there's simply an unsettled feeling deep in your gut. A feeling that tells you something isn't right. A feeling that prods you to question whether there's more to life than this.

That's where hope comes in.

A glimmer of hope is like lighting a match in a dark room. It may begin as a small flame, but mixed with the right fuel, it has the potential to spread, filling the chamber with both warmth and light.

Where do you find hope? Have you found it?

My Life

I feel like I'm important as a mother. I'm showing people that a young mother is totally capable of raising a baby and finishing high school. I've also faced other challenges. I was diagnosed with anaplastic large-cell lymphoma when my daughter was three months old. I had to drop out of school my second semester and undergo six rounds of chemo while still raising a baby. I have now finished high school and will graduate with my class in May. I feel as though I have shown those around me that you can overcome challenges and make it.

— Desiree, *Texas*

Happily Ever After

> *Prince Henry: Will you meet me tomorrow?*
> *Danielle: I shall try.*
> *Prince Henry: Then I shall wait all day.*

— From the movie *Ever After*

I love fairy tales. In fact, *Ever After*, a classic Cinderella story starring Drew Barrymore, is one of my favorite movies. It's a story about a common girl who becomes a princess. The prince not only finds Danielle and carries her away from a life of despair, he also adores her.

The Cinderella story has been retold in different ways through the years. In one movie, the woman is a prostitute and the hero is a wealthy businessman. In another, she is a maid and he is a political candidate. In another, she is the homely daughter of Greek parents and he is a dashing American.

Of course, before the "falling in love" part can happen, there's usually some type of transformation that happens within the main character. In Cinderella's case, her darling fairy godmother sweeps in and transforms her ashes into beauty. In *My Big Fat Greek Wedding*, Toula got a makeover and ditched the nerdy glasses. Then she squared her shoulders, realized her worth, and made up her mind to be the person Ian saw her to be.

How many of us wish we could be written into a fairy tale?
"Once upon a time …"
"A long-ago time, in a faraway land …"
"They lived happily ever after."

To Love and Be Loved

*Sometimes I feel there's a hole inside of me. An emptiness that at
times seems to burn … I have this dream of being whole. Not going
to bed each night wanting. But still sometimes, when the wind is
warm or the crickets sing, I dream of a love that even time will lie
down and be still for.*

— From the movie *Practical Magic*

From as long as I could remember I've wanted to love and be loved.
It was my dream for every relationship I'd ever been in. From first
glance, I wanted to be swept away and adored. I wanted what happened a long time ago in a faraway land to happen to me. Today.
Right where I was. And it did.

My Life

My hope lies in God alone. He has shown me how he can take a
steel heart and slowly melt it down. Without God I would probably
be out living a single lifestyle — without a husband or God. I would be
destroying myself and my kids.

— Laticia, *Oklahoma*

Here's another story of hope from another young mom.

"My story is kind of different from others. I was passed back
and forth from my mom to my grandparents for most of my young
life. My mom loved being my friend. It was the mom part she had a
problem with. I always felt like I had to take care of her, telling her
what was right and wrong.

"When I was thirteen, I decided it was time for me to have a baby of my own. I was very mature for my age, and I almost envied other young moms. I thought to myself, *They are so cool. If only that was me.*

"So when I was one month away from my fourteenth birthday, I met a guy and decided I would stop my birth control. (Yes, I had birth control at thirteen). Well, it worked, but I had a miscarriage and was devastated. Still, my boyfriend and I stayed together and got married. Three weeks after the honeymoon, I found out I was pregnant again. I was so happy.

"Then came the fear. What if I can't finish school, or what if I can't take care of the baby? I vowed to finish high school and not let my pregnancy change anything.

"All this time I had wanted to be pregnant, but when it happened I started to realize things don't always happen the way we imagine. I had always thought I was grown up, but I was in for an awakening. I had to become a twenty-five-year-old woman overnight. It took some time—and the Lord—to help me mature.

"When I was pregnant, I would be in Wal-Mart and the older women would look and shake their heads. The only way I was able to get through the looks and whispers was my confidence in Christ. I can lift my head because the closer I came to him, the better I became. I don't think I would even be married today if it wasn't for Christ. He has been my strength.

"People always seem to have pity on me and feel sorry for me. But that is only at first. After they talk to me for a while, they see I am not some little girl who doesn't know what she's doing. God gives all of us a purpose and for three years I was looking for mine. God made me a mom. I have found my importance through God. He's given me hope."[2]

Hope Is a Person

Hope is a person, and his name is Jesus Christ. I don't know what that name means to you. Perhaps you've heard it used as a curse word. Perhaps you connect it with people who've told you they were

Christians but hurt you deeply. Thankfully, Jesus is big enough to stand on his own two feet. He was a living, breathing person who came to earth with a mission. I'll try to explain it simply.

Jesus was present at the creation of the world. The most prized of all his creation was humankind. God gave man and woman a choice to obey or disobey. They chose the latter, and sin entered into the world. This was no surprise to Jesus. From the beginning, he knew what he would be asked to do.

Thousands of years passed from the time God created the earth until Jesus walked on it, but God was not silent.

He spoke to men and women about freedom from their sins. He spoke in words and through the examples of people's lives. Prophets foretold God coming to earth as man. Believers in God pictured a powerful ruler who would conquer their enemies. Instead, Jesus was far from powerful, if judged in earthly terms. He was not a military ruler. He did not live in a king's castle. In fact, Jesus was born to an unmarried, teen mother.

He was a simple man, a carpenter, who liked to hang out with friends. He liked to talk to people about God in a way they understood. He talked to them through stories.

Jesus hung out with people the religious considered "dirty." He had dinner with prostitutes. His best buddies were uneducated fishermen. He happily spent time with the young moms of the day.

From the time of creation until the days of Jesus' life, God showed his followers a way for men and women to pay for their sins. The only way was to sacrifice an innocent lamb. The lamb's death paid for people's sins—sins that were worthy of death.

When Jesus came to earth, he was prepared to pay the price once and for all. Jesus became the sacrificial lamb, and this too was planned from the beginning. Jesus' death conquered sin. And when he rose from the dead three days later, he conquered death.

We too can conquer death when we have faith in what the Bible says: that Jesus is the way to God.

John 3:16 says, "This is how much God loved the world: He gave his Son, his one and only Son. And this is why: so that no one need be destroyed; by believing in him, anyone can have a whole and lasting life" (MSG).

All you have to do is believe. Tell him you believe, and your life will change—like my life and the lives of so many others. It just takes one prayer like this:

> *Dear Lord Jesus, I believe that you are the prince I have always dreamed of and that you love me completely. I also believe that I was created with an inner desire that only you can fill. I need your help. I need the eternal life only you can give. I want to trust you as my Savior. Please accept my prayer. I welcome you into my life. I'm ready to start a relationship with you that will last for my lifetime and beyond. Amen.*

If you prayed that prayer as you read it, you can be sure that your life will never be the same! You have reason to hope, not just for good things in this life but also for an eternity with God. You can also be sure that Jesus will assist you in meeting your needs as you walk through life with him.

What a Relationship with Jesus Is All About

It may be hard for you to understand what it means to have a relationship with someone you can't see or touch. When you start any relationship, one of the first things you do is spend time together.

Spending time with Jesus includes reading the Bible, communicating with him in prayer, and watching in eager anticipation to see what he's doing in your life. It's not easy at first. But remember that it's the beginning of your relationship, the beginning of something new. The more you interact with Jesus, the more you'll want to:

Read the Bible. The Bible is made up of two sections, the Old Testament and the New Testament. The Old Testament begins with creation and follows the story of God's interaction with people up until four hundred years before Jesus walked on earth.

The New Testament begins with the story of Jesus in the first four books: Matthew, Mark, Luke, and John. It continues by telling about the first Christians and their struggles and triumphs while following Jesus. The New Testament ends with prophecies about the end of earth as we know it.

The Bible is made up of many types of literature. There is poetry, such as in the book of Psalms; prophecy, such as in the book of Isaiah; and eyewitness reports, such as in the book of John. There also are letters, such as the book of Romans.

There are all styles of Bibles for you to choose from. There are study Bibles that have additional information about the text. There are teen Bibles that have added sections on things that concern young people. There are even Bibles put together especially for moms. These Bibles highlight verses that are useful in parenting. They also have supplemental stories and quotes to encourage you in your mothering. There are also various translations, such as *The Message*, that are written in today's language and are easier to understand.

When you begin to study the Bible, the best place to start is the New Testament, especially the first four books—Matthew, Mark, Luke, and John—which describe Jesus' life on earth. Start by simply reading. Get a feel for the words and the flow. Follow what Jesus did and said. Some stories may seem exciting or amazing. Others may be sad or confusing. Some may even seem strange. But keep reading. It's his way of showing us who he is. What a gift!

Pray. Prayer is simply talking with God. You don't have to know any "correct" words or memorize long passages. You can simply tell God how you feel, praise him for what he's doing, and ask him to help you. You can also ask forgiveness when you blow it. Also, no matter what you've seen on TV, you don't have to get on your knees to pray. You can if you want to, but God hears you just the same when you're in bed or jogging through your neighborhood.

Spend time with other Christians. The Bible instructs us to spend time with other people who follow Jesus. They help to encourage and support us. More experienced Christians are also able to answer our questions by showing us truths in the Bible.

The best place to meet Christians is at church. I know, for some of you that seems like the last place you want to go. Maybe there are church people who have hurt you. Maybe there are church people who have judged you. I've had both happen to me. Of course, I've also had church people pour love on me—love I didn't deserve or expect. My advice is to look around for someone you trust—maybe a coworker, a neighbor, or a friend. Ask that person about her church. Ask if you can join her sometime. It's hard to go into a church all alone, especially when all those eyes are on you. And if you don't know someone who goes to church, ask God to show you where to turn.

My cousin Melissa was also a single mom, and she prayed that God would show her how to get closer to him. She worked as a waitress, and one man would always leave her a nice note and a big tip. One day he also left her a business card with his name and information about the church where he was a pastor. She and her boyfriend soon started attending. They trusted the man, and he was happy to see Melissa there. He led her around and introduced her to others from his congregation. Those people became important in Melissa's life, all because she prayed.

We don't have to be on this journey by ourselves. Ask God to lead you to a Bible-believing church that will inspire and encourage you. Also know that God's church is more than just a place to visit on Sundays. The church is also the people who join together to share God's love with the world.

Notice when God is at work in your life. One of the best ways to know God is to see what he is doing in your life. Keep a journal of the blessings. God takes care of you in many ways. He loves to love you. You just need to have an open heart to see what he's up to.

Hope for All Your Situations

As we look back at the needs discussed in this book, you can see how hope was the final piece.

Do I Matter? (Importance) You do matter, you know. The first chapter discussed many reasons why. We discussed why being a good mom is important, especially because of the impact you have on your child. But when it comes to your relationship with God, what matters most is how God sees you. You are significant, not because of what you do, but because of who you are. Once you realize your worth to God, you are free to be the mom he designed you to be.

Who Am I? (Identity) You are God's special creation. He designed you exactly the way he wanted you, and he loves you just as you are. When you see yourself as God sees you, you don't have to worry about an identity crisis. You are his child. His creation. Trust, rest, and rejoice in the person he made you to be.

Where Am I Going? (Growth) If you could see the potential God has planted inside you, there'd be no holding you back! When you take time to explore your dreams and dare to grow by trusting God to help you, you become more of the person he designed you to be. You also become a gift to those around you, including your child.

Do You Love Me? (Intimacy) When discussing intimacy, we talked about connecting with someone who touches your heart—through communication, time spent together, and love shared. When it comes to perfect love and perfect intimacy, there is only one person who can meet your every need. Only God's love is perfect. Only he can satisfy your deepest longings. God, as Jesus Christ, came to earth to show us what this love was all about. When you decide to embark on a relationship with Jesus, you will discover that his intimacy reaches a place no human can touch.

How Do I Do This Mom Thing? (Instruction) The Bible is the ultimate source of instruction. Jesus says in John 14:6, "I am the way and the truth and the life. No one comes to the Father except through me." When we follow Jesus' instructions, we will find the right path for the future. We will discover truth. And we will discover the joy only God can give.

Can You Help? (Help) Sometimes we want God to whisk us out of difficult situations like a rescue helicopter. But honestly, most of the time he lets us struggle through the difficulties. Why? He knows our problems help us to grow. It's how we learn to trust him more. And he loves us enough to want us to depend on him and to seek him out for help.

If we ask for his help, God never makes us struggle alone. His help may be bringing another person into our life. It may be giving us the courage to deal with our bad habits or to get out of a destructive relationship. His help may be providing the strength to attend school, to work, and to take care of a baby. Jesus is available 24/7. Just ask.

Can I Have a Break? (Recreation) When God created the world, he worked for six days, then rested on the seventh. He didn't need to take that long. He didn't need a day off. He did it as an example for us. God created within us the need to balance our work with rest. This includes a physical breather—actually setting aside a day for recreation. We don't need to feel guilty for the way we were made. Taking time for recreation is just as important as taking time to meet our other needs!

What's Most Important? (Perspective) Perspective means focusing on what will last, especially our family and our other relationships. As we focus on God, he shows us what's important. He will point out the things that will last forever. They are the things we will never regret giving our time, energy, and love to.

What Am I Here For? (Hope) Finally we end with hope. Hope is a person by the name of Jesus. Hope is a person who will never leave you. Hope will change everything.

Being a mom isn't easy, but knowing that Jesus is there will make all the difference. On this earth you may find a good man to marry. I hope you do! But there is more to life than this earth. If you accept Jesus, if you seek him and love him, he will be waiting in eternity for you. He will usher you into his kingdom. He will escort you into your forever home, heaven.

This is important for you as a mom, but it's also important for your child. When you have hope, you can pass it on. When you have Jesus, you can pass on your faith in him, and your child's life will be forever changed. Your child's eternity will be forever changed too.

It's the best gift a mother can give, one that will last forever.

And sometimes, because of God's kindness, he chooses to bless us here on earth too. Here is the rest of the story.

Prince Charming Arrives

In an amazing way that I never expected, God brought a wonderful man into my life. My mom received a phone call the day Cory was born. I went home the same day I had him and was sitting on the couch holding my baby when the phone rang. It was my grandma telling me that John Goyer was coming over. That was my pastor's name, so I didn't think much about it.

Not too long after the call, there was a knock at the door. It was not my pastor. It was another John Goyer—his son. His handsome son who played the drums at church. He brought a card for me and a teddy bear for Cory. It was the sweetest gesture! A few weeks later John asked me out on a date. He was handsome and intelligent. He was fun to be with. He was everything I'd hoped for. Soon John made it clear that he cared for me. He also cared for my son.

Yet as wonderful as John is, he is not my prince charming. He—like any person—has his flaws. John is a man, and he will never be perfect. His love will never be perfect.

There is someone else who loves me perfectly. He always has my best in mind. He is looking forward to loving me forever. His name is Jesus.

Do you long for a Prince Charming? The prince you've always longed for is Jesus. He is our hope. He is our prince who will never fail us.

Did you know that my Cinderella story can be your Cinderella story too?

Jesus not only wants to be my Prince Charming, he also wants to be yours.

My Cinderella story doesn't have to be unique to me. Do you want to find meaning and fulfillment in your life? Do you want something to look forward to? Do you want a relationship that will never end? Do you want a love that will last forever?

Friend, you don't need a fairy godmother. You don't need a pumpkin that turns into a carriage or mice that turn into horses and horsemen. You don't have to show up at a ball and dance with grace.

You don't have to dance at all. Jesus will come to you wherever you are. Jesus will take you just as you are, and he'll love you. He'll love you just as you are, forever.

He's Asking You to Dance

Read the following poem. Imagine yourself dancing with Jesus.

The Dance

Are you ready for the embrace of a lifetime?
We have a choice every day, you and I.
And it's a choice we make every day, throughout the day.
The choice is:
We can dance.
Or we can sit it out.

If we dance, we may step on his toes. And he may step on ours. We may stumble and bump into other people. We may fall on our faces and make fools of ourselves. People may talk, they may avoid us, they may even ridicule us.

If you fear those things, you may want to sit this one out.

If you do, you won't have to worry. You'll be safe in your seat along the wall. You'll also miss the dance.

More important, you'll miss the romance.

At some time or another, I have chosen to sit it out. Fear was a big reason. Fear of the attention it would bring, and perhaps the criticism. Fear of embarrassment and possible estrangement. Fear of not being in control of my life, my career, my future. Fear of being led to places that would be uncomfortable, even painful.

There are two things I have learned from the divine embrace.

Perfect love really does cast out fear.

And I would rather dance poorly with Jesus than sit perfectly with anyone else.

— Ken Gire, *The Divine Embrace*[3]

Prayer Changes Things

Twelve Reasons to Pray

1. It encourages others.
2. It reminds you of spiritual values.
3. It gives you hope.
4. It helps you feel better.
5. It allows you to let go of situations.
6. It provides comfort.
7. It relaxes you and reduces anxiety.
8. It builds faith.
9. It deepens character.
10. It broadens your perspective.
11. It brings you closer to God.
12. It works.[4]

Make your own list of reasons to pray:

ACTS Prayer

When it comes to praying, there's no formula. It is just talking to God. Another thing that's good to know is that there are different types of prayers. So if you're ever at loss for words, an easy thing to remember is ACTS. When your baby is napping today, take some time to journal through an ACTS prayer.

- *Adoration*. This means to worship God and show your love for him. It can go something like this, "God, you are wonderful! You are full of love and goodness!"
- *Confession*. This is the time when you confess the wrongs you have done. They can be big or small. And with your confession, know that God will forgive. Here's an example: "God, forgive me for failing to be loving and patient with others as you have been with me."

- *Thanksgiving*. Just thank God for all that he's given you! "God, thank you for my child, my family, my health, and so many other things that I often take for granted."
- *Supplication* or praying for your needs. Do you need help with school or work? Do you need to find a better job? Do you need help potty-training your child? Ask!

Time to Feed Your Soul

Tips for Reading Your Bible

Just like food nourishes your body, God's Word can feed your soul. Here's how:

- *Preparation*. Before you start, find a quiet place to read where you won't be distracted. Also, ask God to speak to you through his words.
- *Start with small bites*. Don't feel like you have to sit down and read the entire Bible cover to cover. Take small bites, such as fifteen minutes a day. (In fact, if you consistently read for fifteen minutes a day, you will read the whole Bible in one year!)
- *Digest it*. There is a difference between just reading your Bible and really taking it in. To digest God's messages:
  1. Read slowly.
  2. Pause and think about any passages that stir your imagination.
  3. Try to imagine the stories or images in your mind.
  4. Write down any questions you may have. Also, write down any messages that are meaningful to you.
  5. Use study tools found in your Bible to answer your questions. This may include footnotes on the bottom of the page or an index in the back of the book. You can also pick up a good Bible dictionary and study guides in a Bible bookstore or online. If you need more help, ask your mentor or a trusted, godly friend.
- *Put God's Word to work*. Just as food energizes your body, let God's Word energize your life. Memorize short passages by reading them over and over again. Then stop and consider how the passages apply to your

everyday circumstances. You may be surprised by how much you'll be able to apply God's concepts to your life!

- *Share it*. Sharing a meal is always more fun when someone else joins you. Find a partner to read God's Word with you, or perhaps join a Bible study group. Also, write your favorite passages on index cards and pass them out to others who may need encouragement.

Don't Give Up Hope

God's Delays Are Not Denials

What do you hope for? Are you getting discouraged because your prayers aren't getting answered the way you want or as quickly as you'd like? If so, consider the following story.

> Never think that God's delays are God's denials. A lone shipwreck survivor on an uninhabited island managed to build a rude hut in which he placed all that he had saved from his sinking ship. He prayed to God for deliverance, and anxiously watched the horizon each day to hail a passing ship. One day he was horrified to find his hut in flames. All that he had was gone. To the man's limited vision, it was the worst that could happen, and he cursed God. Yet the very next day a ship arrived. "We saw your smoke signal!" the captain told him.[5]

This story just goes to show that in your own life there may be times when it seems all is lost, but you can trust that God has a plan. It's a matter of living by faith, not sight.

Put It to Paper

A Blessing Journal

"Each day comes bearing its gifts. Untie the ribbons," says writer Ann Ruth Schabacker. You can count your blessings and record them by starting a Blessing Journal.

- *Begin*. Start with a blank book or a spiral-bound notebook.
- *Recollect*. Think over the special gifts given to you throughout the day. They can be anything from a baby's smile to extra hours on your paycheck.
- *Record*. Write down a set number of blessings or gifts given to you that day. The end of the day is a good time to do this as you think over the past twenty-four hours. Choose one, three, or five to write down.
- *Focus on the heart*. Don't worry about your handwriting, or that you have a stain from your coffee cup, or even that toddler fingers have left smudge marks. The purpose isn't the words on the page; it's the thankfulness in your heart.
- *Be thankful*. As you write each one of your blessings, realize how important each one is. Also, be sure to thank God for loving you so much.
- *Transform*. Over time you'll notice that recording your blessings changes your attitude from one of despair to one of gratitude.
- *Share*. Give the joy of a Blessing Journal to your friends or family. You can keep it simple or customize it with a picture of you and your baby. You can even sign the front with a special note.

Live and Learn

Hope is a person who loves me completely!

Acknowledgments

Thank you to Amy Lathrop and the Litfuze chicks for being the best assistants anyone can have. Many people ask how I do it all. Thankfully, I don't have to do it all with you on my team!

I also appreciate the Zondervan team, especially Sandra Vander Zicht, Bridget Klein, Brian Phipps, and Alicia Kasen. Your insight and help on this project is appreciated! I also send thanks to all the managers, designers, copy editors, proofreaders, salespeople, financial folks, and everyone else who make a book possible!

I'm also thankful for my agent, Janet Grant. Your wisdom and guidance has made all the difference.

And I'm thankful for my family at home:

- John, I'm so thankful for a husband who believes in me, supports me, and cheers me on.
- Cory, Katie, Clayton, and Chloe: I love to see God at work in your lives!
- Leslie, your passion for young people from around the world is inspiring!
- Nathan, you are a wonder, a gentle soul. I'm so thankful for you.
- Bella, Alyssa, and Casey: What bundles of joy you are! Every day is brighter since God brought you three into our lives!
- My grandma Dolores and my mom, Linda: I'm so thankful for your love for me!
- And to the rest of my family: I appreciate all of you! I'm so thankful you're in my life! God gave me the gift of you!

I'm also thankful for the young women who shared their thoughts and stories in this book:

Kayleigh	Marjie	Simone
Elizabeth	Sarah	Jessica
Diana	Nina	Jamie
Desiree	Katherine	Travis
Amanda	Mari	Laticia

I know your insights will encourage other young moms!

Finally, I'm thankful for our Teen MOPS group in Little Rock, Arkansas. You ladies are such a blessing.

Teen MOPS Leaders

Anglita Thomas	Jan Jeffrey	Kia Smith
Kyna Williams	Lori DeYmaz	Samantha Font
Hannah Halfhill	Kayleigh Stoltz	Kim Marshall
Linda Lovett	Misty Jones	

Teen MOPS Young Women

Alina	Elizabeth	Meagan
Ashlee	Janelle	Nikita
Beatriz	Jessika	Tomesha
Christelle	Katie	Tashzeri
Ciara	Katie H.	
Corbin	Liana	

God has big plans for you ladies!

Notes

Introduction: Me ... A Mom?

1. Not her real name.
2. Not her real name.
3. Joyce A. Martin et al., "Births: Final Data for 2012," *National Vital Statistics Reports* 62, no. 9 (Dec. 30, 2013). Retrieved January 21, 2014, from *http://www.cdc.gov/nchs/data/nvsr/nvsr62/nvsr62_09.pdf*.
4. Ibid.
5. K. Welti, "Percentage of Teens Who Will Experience a First Birth, Based on Analyses of NCHS Vital Statistics 2010 Final Birth Data," unpublished manuscript.
6. Bradley E. Hamilton, PhD, and Stephanie J. Ventura, MA, "Birth Rates for U.S. Teenagers Reach Historic Lows for All Age and Ethnic Groups," *NCHS Data Brief* no. 89 (April 2012), *http://www.cdc.gov/nchs/data/databriefs/db89.htm*, accessed September 10, 2014.

Chapter 1: Do I Matter?

1. Author unknown, quoted in Jack Canfield et al., *Chicken Soup for the Mother's Soul* (Deerfield Beach, FL: Health Communications, 2001), 95.
2. William Sears et al., from *Parent Project: Tools for Godly Parenting* quoted in Alice Gray, Steve Stephens, and John van Diest, comps., *Lists to Live By for Every Caring Family* (Sisters, OR: Multnomah, 2001), 107. Used with permission.

Chapter 2: Who Am I?

1. Jay McGraw, *Life Strategies for Teens Workbook* (New York: Simon and Schuster, 2001), 52.
2. Elisa Morgan and Carol Kuykendall, *What Every Mom Needs* (Grand Rapids, MI: Zondervan, 1995), 44.

Chapter 3: Where Am I Going?

1. Dannah Gresh, *Secret Keeper: The Delicate Power of Modesty* (Chicago: Moody, 2002), 23.

Chapter 4: Do You Love Me?

1. Lawrence B. Finer and Jesse M. Philbin, "Sexual Initiation, Contraceptive Use, and Pregnancy among Young Adolescents," *Pediatrics* 131, no. 5 (April 21, 2013), *doi:10.1542\peds.2012-3495*, accessed May 31, 2013.
2. Michael Hodgin, *1001 Humorous Illustrations for Public Speaking* (Grand Rapids, MI: Zondervan, 1994), 229. Used with permission.
3. Jo-Ellen Dimitrius, *Reading People* (New York: Random House, 1998), 13.

4. Heritage Foundation, based on data from the *National Longitudinal Survey of Adolescent Health*, a nationwide survey that examined behaviors of adolescents in junior high and high school (Family Research Council, Press Release, 3 June 2003), *www.frc.org*.
5. Centers for Disease Control and Prevention, "Genital HPV Infection—Fact Sheet," Centers for Disease Control and Prevention website, March 20, 2014, *http://www.cdc.gov/std/hpv/stdfact-hpv.htm*, accessed September 07, 2014.
6. Pam Stenzel, "Sex Has a Price Tag!" *http://www.prolife.com/stenzel.htm*, accessed September 09, 2014.
7. Elisa Morgan, *God's Word of Life for Moms* (Grand Rapids: MI: Zondervan, 2000), 85. Used with permission.
8. Andrea J. Buchanan, *Mother Shock: Tales from the First Year and Beyond* (New York: Seal Press, 2003), 1.
9. Ruth Bell Graham, quoted in Alice Gray, comp., *Stories for the Family's Heart* (Sisters, OR: Multnomah, 1998), 128.
10. Stephanie Pappas, "Early Neglect Alters Kids' Brains," LiveScience, July 23, 2012, *http://www.livescience.com/21778-early-neglect-alters-kids-brains.html*, accessed September 09, 2014.
11. Elisa Morgan and Carol Kuykendall, *What Every Mom Needs* (Grand Rapids, MI: Zondervan, 1995), 87.
12. Carole Mayhall, condensed from *Lord, Teach Me Wisdom*, quoted in Alice Gray, Steve Stephens, and John van Diest, comps., *Lists to Live By for Everything That Really Matters* (Sisters, OR: Multnomah, 1999), 123. Used with permission.
13. Al Gray and Alice Gray, quoted in *Lists to Live By for Everything That Really Matters*, compiled by Alice Gray, Steve Stephens, and John van Diest (Sisters, OR: Multnomah, 1999), 119. Used with permission.

Chapter 5: How Do I Do This Mom Thing?

1. Andrea J. Buchanan, *Mother Shock: Tales from the First Year and Beyond* (New York: Seal Press, 2003), 54.
2. Charles R. Swindoll, *Growing Strong in the Seasons of Life*, (Grand Rapids, MI: Zondervan, 1983), 290. Used with permission.
3. Patti MacGregor, from "Family Times: Growing Together in Fun and Faith," quoted in Alice Gray, Steve Stephens, and John van Diest, comps., *Lists to Live By for Everything That Really Matters* (Sisters, OR: Multnomah, 1999), 313. Used with permission.
4. Robert Bender, *Never Eat Anything That Moves: Good, Bad, and Very Silly Advice from Kids* (New York: Dial Books for Young Readers, 2002).
5. Author unknown, quoted in Alice Gray, Steve Stephens, and John van Diest, comps., *Lists to Live By for Everything That Really Matters* (Sisters, OR: Multnomah, 1999), 315.

Chapter 6: Can You Help?

1. Julie Ann Barnhill, *She's Gonna Blow! Real Help for Moms Dealing with Anger* (Eugene, OR: Harvest House, 2001), 176.
2. Elisa Morgan, *God's Words of Life for Moms* (Grand Rapids, MI: Inspiro, 2000), 17. Used with permission.
3. Andrea Engber and Leah Klungness, *The Complete Single Mother* (Holbrook, MA: Adams Publishing, 1995), 41.
4. Andrea Engber and Leah Klungness, *The Complete Single Mother* (Holbrook, MA: Adams Publishing, 1995), 99. Copyright © 1995, 2000 Andrea Engber and Leah Klungness. Used with permission of Adams Media. All rights reserved.
5. Dan Clark, quoted in Jack Canfield et al., *Chicken Soup for the Mother's Soul: 101 Stories to Open the Hearts and Rekindle the Spirits of Mothers* (Deerfield Beach, FL: Health Communications, 1997), 203. Used with permission.
6. Brenda Nixon, *www.parentpwr.com*.

Chapter 7: Can I Get a Break?

1. Michael Hodgin, *1001 Humorous Illustrations for Public Speaking* (Grand Rapids, MI: Zondervan, 1994), 316. Used with permission.
2. Copyright © 1997 by Elaine Hardt. Hardt Ministries International, Inc. 4700 Scout Way, Prescott Valley, AZ 86314. Used with permission.
3. Sylvia Harney, *Everytime I Go Home, I Break Out in Relatives* (Nashville: Word, 1990), 123.
4. *Simple Truths for Moms* (Lincolnwood, IL: New Seasons Publishers, 2001), 5.
5. Heather Hurd, Kathy Knight, and Cecil O. Kemp Jr., eds., *A Book of Hope for Mothers* (Nashville: Wisdom Company, 2000).
6. Amanda, Ontario, Canada.
7. Julie Ann Barnhill, *She's Gonna Blow! Real Help for Moms Dealing with Anger* (Eugene, OR: Harvest House, 2001), 176.
8. Simone, New Zealand.
9. Diana, Washington.
10. Travis, Michigan.
11. Travis, Michigan.
12. Diane and Rob Parsons, *The Sixty Minute Mother* (Nashville: Broadman and Holman, 2002), 102. Used with permission.
13. Karyn Henley, from *HomeLife Magazine*, quoted in Alice Gray, Steve Stephens, and John van Diest, comps., *Lists to Live By for Every Caring Family* (Sisters, OR: Multnomah, 2001), 68–69. Used with permission.

Chapter 8: What's Most Important?

1. Michael Hodgin, 1001 Humorous Illustrations for Public Speaking (Grand Rapids, MI: Zondervan, 1994), 642. Used with permission.
2. Lucinda Bassett, Life without Limits (New York: Cliff Street Books, 2001), 187.
3. Author unknown, quoted in Alice Gray, Steve Stephens, and John van Diest, comps., Lists to Live By for Everything That Really Matters (Sisters, OR: Multnomah, 1999), 317.
4. Joanna Weaver, Having a Mary Heart in a Martha World (Colorado Springs, CO: WaterBrook, 2002), 184.
5. Sark, Succulent Wild Woman: Dancing with Your Wonder-Full Self (New York: Simon and Schuster, 1997), 117.
6. Author unknown, Alice Gray, comp., Stories for the Family's Heart (Sisters, OR: Multnomah, 1998), 179.

Chapter 9: What Am I Here For?

1. Emily Dickinson, Selected Poems and Letters of Emily Dickenson, Robert N. Linscott, ed. (Garden City: Doubleday Anchor, 1959), 79.
2. Laticia, Oklahoma.
3. Ken Gire, The Divine Embrace: An Invitation to the Dance of Intimacy with Christ One Exhilarating, Ennobling, Uncertain Step at a Time (Carol Stream, IL: Tyndale, 2003). Used with permission.
4. John van Diest, quote in Alice Gray, Steve Stephens, and John van Diest, comps., Lists to Live By for Everything That Really Matters (Sisters, OR: Multnomah, 1999), 206. Used with permission.
5. Michael Hodgin, 1001 Humorous Illustrations for Public Speaking (Grand Rapids, MI: Zondervan, 1994), 642. Used with permission.

Credits

The material in chapter 1 titled "Messages for Baby" is taken from William Sears, Martha Sears, Joyce Warmna, et al., *Parent Project: Tools for Godly Parenting* (Nashville: LifeWay, 2000). Used with permission.

The material in chapters 4 and 6 quoting God's Words of Life for Moms is taken from *God's Words of Life for Moms* by Elisa Morgan. Copyright 2000 by the Zondervan Corporation. Used by permission of the Zondervan Corporation.

The material in chapters 4, 7, and 8 quoting 1001 *Humorous Illustrations for Public Speaking* is taken from 1001 *Humorous Illustrations for Public Speaking* by Michael Hodgin. Copyright 1994 by Michael Hodgin. Used by permission of the Zondervan Corporation.

The material in chapter 4 titled "Springboards to Deeper Conversation" is condensed from Carole Mayhall, *Lord, Teach Me Wisdom* (Colorado Springs, Colo.: NavPress, 1979). Used with permission.

The material in chapter 4 titled "Eighteen Attributes to Look for in a Marriage Partner" is from Al Gray and Alice Gray, quoted in *Lists to Live By for Everything That Really Matters*, compiled by Alice Gray, Steve Stephens, and John van Diest (Sisters, Ore.: Multnomah, 1999). Used with permission.

The material in chapter 5 quoting *Growing Strong in the Seasons of Life* is taken from *Growing Strong in the Seasons of Life* by Charles R. Swindoll. Copyright 1983 by Charles R. Swindoll, Inc. Used by permission of the Zondervan Corporation.

The material in chapter 5 titled "Wise Things Your Grandma Told You" is from Patti MacGregor, "Family Times: Growing Together in Fun and Faith," quoted in *Lists to Live By for Everything That Really Matters* (Sisters, Ore.: Multnomah, 1999). Used with permission.

The material in chapter 6 titled "The Broken Doll" is taken from Dan Clark, quoted in *Chicken Soup for the Mother's Soul: 101 Stories to Open the Hearts and Rekindle the Spirits of Mothers* (Deerfield Beach, Fla.: Health Communications, 1997), 203. Used with permission.

The material in chapter 6 titled "Handling Feelings about an Uninvolved Father" is from *The Complete Single Mother*. Copyright © 1995, 2000 Andrea Engber and Leah Klungness. Used with permission of Adams Media. All rights reserved.

The poem in chapter 7 titled "Make a Memory" by Elaine Hardt is © 1977 by Elaine Hardt, Hardt Ministries International, Inc. 4700 Scout Way, Prescott Valley, AZ 86314. Used with permission.

The material in chapter 7 quoted from Diane and Rob Parsons, *The 60 Minute Mother* (Nashville: Broadman and Holman, 2002) is used with permission.

The material in chapter 7 titled "Just for Fun" is used with permission of Karyn Henley.

The material in chapter 9 titled "The Dance" is taken from Ken Gire, *The Divine Embrace* (Carol Stream, Ill.: Tyndale, 2003). Used with permission.

The material in chapter 9 titled "Twelve Reasons to Pray" is from John van Diest, quoted in *Lists to Live By for Everything That Really Matters*, compiled by Alice Gray, Steve Stephens, and John van Diest (Sisters, Ore.: Multnomah, 1999). Used with permission.

For Further Reading

The Mom You're Meant to Be, by Cheri Fuller

God's Words of Life for Moms, by Elisa Morgan

Life Strategies for Teens, by Jay McGraw

Mother Shock, by Andrea J. Buchanan

Reading People, by Jo-Ellan Dimitrius

What Every Mom Needs, by Elisa Morgan and Carol Kuykendall